about the author

KITTY BROIHIER, MS, RD, is the president of NutriComm, a food and nutrition communications consulting company serving food companies and public relations firms. Ms. Broihier is coauthor of *The Everything Vitamins, Minerals, and Nutritional Supplements Book* (Adams Media, 2001), and *The Everyday Low-Carb Slow Cooker Cookbook* (Marlowe & Co., 2004). Previously an editor at *Good Housekeeping* magazine, Ms. Broihier is the author of many magazine articles and contributes regularly to a variety of publications, including *Parenting, Shape, Cooking Light, Health, Environmental Nutrition* newsletter, and *Weight Watchers Magazine.*

A registered dietitian, Ms. Broihier received a bachelor's of science degree in dietetics from Michigan State University, and a master's of science degree in Nutrition Communications from Boston University. She is a member of the American Dietetic Association, and is a founding member of the ADA's Food and Culinary Professionals practice group. Ms. Broihier resides in South Portland, Maine, with her husband and two young children.

everyday low-carb desserts

low-carb *everyday* desserts

OVER 120 DELICIOUS LOW-CARB TREATS PERFECT FOR ANY OCCASION

• Kitty Broihier, MS, RD •

MARLOWE & COMPANY
NEW YORK

EVERYDAY LOW-CARB DESSERTS:
Over 120 Delicious Low-Carb Treats Perfect for Any Occasion

Published by
Marlowe & Company
An Imprint of Avalon Publishing Group Incorporated
245 West 17th Street • 11th floor
New York, NY 10011

AVALON
publishing group incorporated

Library of Congress Cataloging-in-Publication Data
Broihier, Kitty,
Everyday low-carb desserts : over 120 delicious low-carb treats perfect for any
occasion / by Kitty Broihier.
p. cm.
Includes index.
ISBN 1-56924-420-0
1. Desserts. 2. Low-carbohydrate diet—Recipes. I. Title.
TX773.B8 2004
641.8'6—dc22
20004058181

9 8 7 6 5 4 3 2 1

Designed by Pauline Neuwirth, Neuwirth and Associates, Inc.

Printed in the United States of America
Distributed by Publishers Group West

For my children, Jack and Amelia, my sweetest creations

contents

foreword

AS YOU MIGHT suspect, the impetus for me to write this book was my own love of sweets. Ask anyone who knows me even remotely and they'll tell you that, despite my lower-carb diet, I haven't lost my sweet tooth. Which leads me to the second reason I wanted to write this book—most low-carb diet plans tend to skimp on the dessert chapter! I'm sure you've noticed that, aside from various berry creations or weird ricotta cheese–based concoctions, most low-carb cookbooks downplay desserts. It's as if, once you go low-carb, desserts—and all your desire for them—will just disappear. For me, going low-carb did diminish my cravings for regular sugar "fixes," but my desire for an occasional decadent dessert did not go away completely. And once in a while I still want to bake something nice for my family or guests—and I want to be able to enjoy it right along with them. To me, that's not asking for too much. If you've purchased this book, you likely agree.

Granted, there are low-carb dessert-type products available commercially, as well as low-carb candies and the like, but when I'm yearning for a warm-from-the-oven, home-baked goodie, no straight-from-the-package sweet will do. What's more, I like to bake. I find it pleasurable and gratifying in many ways. I've been baking on my own since I was about twelve years old (though at early ages what I did was more like helping my sisters and mother bake—mostly I licked the beaters, greased baking sheets, stirred dough, and ate the resulting goodies—still, I was assisting in some capacity!).

When I had my own kids, I began to bake regularly and included them in the process often. My kids could both crack eggs like a short-order diner cook at age three. However, when I began my own, self-devised low-carb diet, I cut back drastically on the home-baking. It was just too hard to bake and then not eat the treats right along with them. I guess you could say that during the low-carb year prior to working on this book, I was in a state of baking "withdrawal."

Not anymore! In this book, you'll find a large selection of desserts ranging from easy, weeknight-type treats (such as Quick Pumpkin Pudding or Mocha Drop Cookies) to more involved, special sweets such as Chocolate Chunk Baked Alaska and Milk Chocolate-Almond Soufflé for Two. Because many of us want to serve our families and friends something special for seasonal holidays and celebrations, I've included a large chapter of "Seasonal Specialties" as well. Finally, you'll find a variety of different types of desserts, from frozen to chocolate, fruit to pudding, and cookies to cakes, plus all the little extras (like flavored whipped creams, raspberry coulis, and hot fudge) that you need to present your desserts with style and great taste.

I hope this book fulfills any dessert cravings you may have—without, of course, sabotaging your low-carb regimen. So dust off your rolling pin, bring your cake pans out of storage, and meet me in the kitchen!

—Kitty Broihier, MS, RD

introduction

BECAUSE I'M A dietitian, I think I get held to a "higher standard" than others when it comes to the food I eat. That's to be expected, I suppose, just as I expect my physician to be fit and healthy, and my dental hygienist to have great-looking teeth. However, the fact that people are surprised when they hear that I eat (or even "catch" me eating) dessert never ceases to amaze me. I'm human, too! I have sweet-taste receptors just like you, and I like chocolate just as much as the next gal!

No doubt, this book will really cement my reputation as a rather "lenient" dietitian. That's okay with me, because I truly believe that food should be enjoyed, savored, and shared with those we care for—not viewed strictly as fuel for the body, or as a prescription for a healthy body. Cooking for friends or family is an act of love, so to me, it follows that taking it one step further by making a nice dessert shows people that they're worth the extra effort. Of course, the fact that I find dessert-making an extremely pleasurable, creative process is also part of the reason that no guests ever leave my dinner table without having been offered some sort of dessert!

• MY "DESSERT PHILOSOPHY" •

IT'S A COMMON dietitian's adage that "all foods can fit," meaning that every food can be worked into a healthful diet, as long as moderation is practiced. Unfortunately, that doesn't mesh too well with the popular low-carb eating plans. Living low-carb—or even just cutting back on carbohydrates—leaves little room for chocolate chip cookies or brownies. And certainly there are some foods that definitely won't *ever* fit in a low-carb eating plan. How do I bring these two positions together? It's not that difficult, but it does mean making some concessions on both sides, which are explained in the sections following.

Working on these recipes has been such an eye-opener for me (and for the folks who taste-tested the recipes), there can be amazing diversity and quality in the low-carb dessert world. There's no reason to choke down less-than-wonderful dessert substitutes, or packaged low-carb sweets that you don't really enjoy. Real, honest-to-goodness desserts can still have a place in a low-carb eating plan, but they have to be planned and properly portioned.

• PLANNING YOUR DESSERTS •

WE ALL KNOW what happens when we're hungry and don't have much around to make a meal out of—we grab whatever looks best, no matter what it is or whether it fits into our eating plan. Low-carb dieters are no different. The problem is, when it comes to desserts, if it's there (even if it's a low-carb dessert), you might be tempted to make a meal out of it in a moment of desperation. Obviously, this isn't good for a variety of reasons; principal among them is the fact that most desserts aren't packed with nutrients. A couple of low-carb cookies are not a good substitute for a decent breakfast; a slice of low-carb pie can't take the place of a dinner entrée nutritionally. If you've planned dessert for an occasion, without a great many leftovers, it's much easier to stick to a more nutritious low-carb diet.

Second, desserts are delightful "extras." They're not everyday fare. Your low-carb diet will be harder to maintain if you eat big desserts daily, and you may find your sweet tooth coming back with a vengeance if the bulk of your diet is made up of sweet (yet low-carb) foods such as meal replacement bars, shakes, and desserts. One low-carb chocolate truffle per day may be fine for you, while a generous portion of cheesecake may prove problematic to your overall efforts. There are also the potential gastrointestinal problems to consider. Too many sugar alcohols can lead to bloating, gas, and diarrhea. Sugar alcohols sweeten many sugar-free and low-carb foods and ingredients. I've used a number of ingredients in this book that contain sugar alcohols. (There are alternatives, but so far many food manufacturers aren't making use of them.) Some people can tolerate quite large amounts of sugar alcohols; others can't. Just be aware that eating too many low-carb sweets can come back to haunt you the next day!

To summarize, if you plan for dessert on occasion—when you have something to celebrate, when you have company coming for dinner, or even just because you want to start a once-a-week dessert tradition in your house—you can easily do so without doing damage to your low-carb lifestyle.

• PORTION CONTROL •

EARLY LOW-CARB eating plans often failed to emphasize moderate portion sizes, which led people to think that, just because a food is low in carbs, they could eat as much of it as they liked and still lose weight. This line of thinking generally works fine with salad greens and vegetables, but not with many other foods.

Because desserts are treats, keeping the portion sizes reasonable is important. Like regular desserts, many low-carb desserts are high in calories and/or fat—something to keep in mind if you're trying to drop pounds. All the desserts in this book list the number of servings the recipe yields. The nutritional information listed is for one portion only (unless otherwise specified). If you alter the number of servings per recipe (by making the servings too large, for example), the nutrition information will no longer be accurate. So, if a recipe is supposed to serve eight and you only get six portions out of it, you'll need to adjust the nutritional information accordingly.

One very important point to note regarding portions sizes: unlike some other low-carb cookbooks I've seen, the portion-sizes for my desserts are not unrealistically tiny. Making portion sizes very small is definitely one way some people keep the carb levels down on their desserts, but it's not a technique that I employ. My thinking is that if you've planned to have a dessert, you ought to have a dessert—not merely a taste. So remember, if you cut the dessert (or apportion it) into the specified number of servings per recipe, your portion will be reasonable and satisfying, and the nutritional information will be correct.

about this book

ALTHOUGH THIS BOOK was created for people following a low-carb eating plan, there's no reason at all why those who aren't "low-carbing" couldn't enjoy these recipes as well. In fact, all of these recipes were tested on people who are not on low-carb diets. My children, neighbors, husband, and friends all helped me test these recipes, and none of them live a low-carb lifestyle. Yet, I never heard any complaints (though constructive criticism was always welcomed). In fact, I took a few of these desserts to parties at other peoples' houses and never advertised the fact that they were low-carb—and not once did anyone say "This tastes like a diet dessert," or "I can tell this is low-carb." To me, that says it all because, while I wanted the recipes to be suitable for low-carbers, I certainly didn't want them to taste any different than "regular" desserts.

Before you begin cooking, there are a few things you ought to know about the recipes in this book, which will help you decide which recipes are appropriate for your eating plan, as not all of them may be suitable for you.

• THE NUTRITIONAL ANALYSIS OF THE RECIPES •

I PROVIDED THE "approximate" nutritional content of each recipe, specifying calories, protein, net carbs, fat, cholesterol, and sodium for one serving of the dessert. The reason I say "approximate" is because, although I've used a well-regarded nutritional analysis program ("Food Processor" by Esha Research), no nutritional analysis can be perfect. There are just too many variables that enter into the cooking of a food—even when the recipe is followed to the letter—for any nutritional analysis to be 100 percent accurate. For example, human error in measurement of ingredients, variations between different brands of ingredients, and even significant differences between nutritional analysis program values for the same food can all affect the analysis. Therefore, although I've done my best to make the nutritional analysis accurate, it still is only an approximation.

To arrive at the nutritional analysis figures, I used "generic" ingredients as often as possible. For example, when a recipe calls for whole-wheat flour or almonds, I've used a generic value. There are certain times, however, when I've used the nutrition information for a specific brand of ingredient, such as chocolate (Repertoire) or preserves (Smucker's sugar-free, "light" preserves). Why? Sometimes only one company makes a particular low-carb or sugar-free product, or sometimes a certain brand of product performs best in the recipe. Plus, I also have some favorite brands, and you'll notice in the "Sources for Low-Carb Dessert Ingredients" chapter (page 11) that I listed some of those products in case you want to try those brands as well.

Finally, when calculating the approximate nutritional content of a recipe, I did not include "optional" ingredients. For example, if a recipe specifies that whipped cream for a garnish is optional, I didn't include it in the analysis. If you want to include those ingredients, you'll need to add their carb values to the total.

⦿ NET CARBS ⦿

WHETHER YOU CALL them "net carbs," "impact carbs," or "effective carbs," they are all basically the same thing; they're the carbs that count when you're following a low-carb eating plan. There is considerable discussion in low-carb circles about how to count carbs for foods that contain sugar alcohols. Some people count the grams of carbohydrates from sugar alcohols partially; others don't count them at all. I've already mentioned that the recipes in this book can contain quite a few sugar alcohols, and now I'll tell you that I'm a member of the second camp—I don't count the sugar alcohol grams at all. In this book I've calculated net carbs using the simple technique I've used in previous low-carb cookbooks, and the one that's employed by food manufacturers for food labeling purposes. It is: Total carbohydrates, minus fiber, minus sugar alcohols equals net carbs. It's my feeling that when desserts (or other foods high in sugar alcohols) are eaten only on occasion, and not on a daily basis, then the few grams of carb contributed by the sugar alcohols won't have a significant impact on overall carbohydrate intake. On the other hand, if one was to eat foods with a high sugar alcohol content several times per day, I would probably suggest that some of those grams of carb be counted toward the daily net carb total.

With a few exceptions, the recipes in this book all fall under 15 grams net carb per serving, and most are considerably less than that. There are desserts here to suit every low-carb eating plan, but it's up to you to determine whether or not a particular recipe is appropriate for your plan.

low-carb dessert basics

• EQUIPMENT •

AS WITH MOST activities in life, having the right equipment is vital for successful dessert-making. In this book I've tried to limit the equipment needs to those pieces that most people with a fairly well-stocked kitchen will already have on hand. Nevertheless, I'll take the time now to remind you to *always* read a recipe through completely before deciding to make it (not to mention reading it before you begin making it). That way you'll know what equipment (and what ingredients) you'll need; if you need anything you don't already own, you'll have time to track it down, borrow it, or purchase it before you're elbow-deep in almond meal and whipped cream!

There are many places to find decent cooking equipment these days. If you don't have a good cookware shop in town, you can usually find quality equipment at department stores, houseware stores, and sometimes even at discount stores. Online cookware Web sites are numerous and convenient, and often have prices equal to or better than storefront retailers. For items that you know you'll be using frequently (for me these include knives, heavy saucepans, and a mixer), it pays to buy quality equipment. Go with well-known brand names (ask a clerk or do some research if you don't know which brands are the most highly regarded), then try to find your best price. If you go the cheap route on these items you can expect to replace them more quickly. For me, replacing cookie sheets and baking pans every year or two is acceptable, because they're readily available and not expensive. On the other hand, buying a new mixer every year is not something I want to do, so I got the best I could find and I haven't been sorry. Think about the types of things you like to cook, and what equipment you're willing to invest in, then make your purchases accordingly.

The following is a list of equipment called for in this book's recipes. Most of the equipment is pretty basic; other items are "specialty" items that are nice to have but not essential. (You can always put those things on your birthday "wish list"—that's how I got my ice-cream maker!)

Pots, pans, and baking dishes

Small, medium, and large saucepans with lids
8-inch square baking pan
9-inch square baking pan
13-by-9-inch baking pan
8-inch round cake pan
9-inch round cake pan
8½-by-3⅓-inch loaf pan (bread pan)
1½-quart casserole dish or baking dish
2-quart casserole dish or baking dish
9-inch pie plate
9-inch tart pan with removable bottom
8-inch springform pan
9-inch springform pan
10-inch springform pan
8-inch round trifle dish
Cookie sheets (shiny metal, not dark, are recommended)
Small, medium, and large mixing bowls

Tools

Sieve
Grater (one that grates both coarse and fine is best)
Whisks (1 large, 1 small)
Dry measuring cups
Measuring cups for liquids (8-ounce and 32-ounce liquid cup)
Measuring spoons
Rolling pin
Wooden spoons
Rubber spatulas (large and small)
Tongs (spring-action ones are best)
Metal spatulas (large and small)
Sharp knives (medium French knife, long serrated knife, small paring knife)
Oven mitts
Oven timer
Wire cooling rack

Electric equipment

Electric mixer (either handheld or a stand mixer)
Small electric food chopper
Blender

Miscellaneous "specialty" equipment

Food processor
"Stick" blender (handheld variety)
Ice-cream maker (I like Cuisinart's)
Kitchen scale

• ABOUT THE INGREDIENTS •

AS I DEVELOPED this book, I came to depend on certain ingredients, which consistently performed well in recipes and were easy to procure. Others I tried once and then abandoned for any of a variety of reasons, including taste, availability, price, and performance. Once I find a dessert ingredient that I love, I'm very loyal to it. Why? In many cases, dessert-making isn't as "forgiving" as regular cooking. For example, one brand of canned black soybeans is very much like another, so I'll generally purchase based on price for these types of ingredients. With baking, however, the chemical reactions of foods are more complicated, measurements have to be more precise, and small differences in ingredient qualities can mean big differences in results. I'm not willing to take chances with my dessert ingredients, because to me there's no settling for a cake that *almost* worked, or a pudding that *almost* set. If it's not right, I won't waste my carbs and calories on it, my family won't eat it, and I've wasted my time and money on something that ended up in the garbage disposal.

That said, I'm happy to notice that nearly every time I go grocery shopping there are new low-carb products on the shelves. Although not all of these products are useful in dessert-making, food manufacturers have clearly responded to consumer demand for increased low-carb food selections, and that's gratifying for all of us who yearn for more variety, more choices, and more ingredients to use in low-carb food preparation.

In general, one doesn't need special packaged low-carb foods in order to adopt a low-carb eating plan. In fact, some people find that the more manufactured foods they eat, the harder it is for them to manage their weight and well-being. However, desserts are one area where, unless you plan to limit yourself to fresh berries and whipped cream for the rest of your days, a few packaged food ingredients are helpful. If you've purchased this book, you've already acknowledged that dessert is important to you, and you're willing to "make room" in your eating plan to allow for these types of products. In my world, having one great dessert a week, which utilizes a few packaged ingredients and includes some sugar alcohols, is completely acceptable (and sometimes crucial in order for me to avoid a feeling of deprivation that might derail my low-carb efforts). This is especially true when I'm having company over or on holidays—I want to be able to join in the fun of eating a special dessert, and if others enjoy my creations too, then all the better!

• MASTERING MEASURING •

MEASURING INGREDIENTS PROPERLY is essential to dessert-making. Because of the various chemical reactions between ingredients, many dessert recipes are not that forgiving—you must measure ingredients correctly or your dessert might not turn out right. After all the time and effort you take to make a dessert, it would be a shame to have it fail simply because you didn't take care when measuring out ingredients. Here are the correct ways to measure ingredients commonly used in this book.

BUTTER: Use a sharp paring knife and cut the sticks at the desired marking on the wrapper.

DRY INGREDIENTS: Stir the flour, Atkins Bake Mix, almond meal, or other dry ingredient in the bag or canister with a large spoon to loosen it. Using a small spoon, scoop the flour into a dry measuring cup until heaping. With the straight side of a butter knife, scrape off any excess flour, leveling the top. Do not shake the cup during measuring, and do not scoop the ingredient with the measuring cup, or it will become compacted and you'll end up with much flour in the recipe. Sifting flour isn't necessary for any of the recipes in this book.

BAKING SODA, BAKING POWDER, SPICES, AND LOW-CARB THICKENERS: Scoop the ingredient with the measuring spoon, then level it off with the straight side of a butter knife.

LIQUIDS: Use measuring cups made for liquids—they'll have a handle and spout on them, and be made of clear plastic or glass. Pour the liquid into the measuring cup on a level surface (not while holding it in your hand), then bend down so that your eyes are level with the measurement markings on the cup (do not read the measurement while standing above the liquid; it's not accurate, unless you have one of the special new "top reading" liquid measuring cups.) When measuring liquids into a measuring spoon, such as with extracts, do not pour the liquids into the spoon over the mixing bowl, in case you spill. Instead, hold the measuring spoon over a custard cup or small bowl, then pour the liquid.

NUTS: In most cases, you should measure the nuts before chopping them. The exception to this is for small quantities of chopped or ground nuts, or for almond meal/flour, which comes already ground.

measurements, equivalents, and conversions

Measurement Equivalents

Dash/pinch	=	less than ⅛ teaspoon
3 teaspoons	=	1 tablespoons
4 tablespoons	=	¼ cup
16 tablespoons	=	1 cup
2 cups	=	1 pint
2 pints	=	1 quart
4 quarts	=	1 gallon
1 fluid ounce	=	2 tablespoons
8 fluid ounces	=	1 cup
16 ounces	=	1 pound

Metric Conversions

Weight:

1 ounce	=	28.4 grams
1 pound	=	454 grams
2.2 pounds	=	1 kilogram

Volume/liquid:

1 teaspoon	=	4.7 milliliters
1 tablespoon	=	14.2 milliliters
1 cup	=	227 milliliters
1.06 quarts	=	1,000 milliliters = 1 liter

sources for low-carb dessert ingredients

$\mathcal{F}$OLLOWING IS A list of ingredients that I've used in this book and recommend. If you find ingredients that you like better than these, by all means use them. If you're just beginning to stock your low-carb pantry, consider this a starting point for dessert ingredients.

Many companies will ship their foods and ingredients directly to you (order online); others can be obtained at a low-carb store, health food or natural foods store, or a general low-carb foods Web site (try lowcarbliving.com, low-carbnexus.com, or just do a search for "low carb foods" to find them).

Grain and nut Products

Arrowhead Mills product line (especially whole wheat pastry flour
    and wheat gluten)
Arrowhead Mills, Inc. (division of The Hain Celestial Group, Inc.)
www.arrowheadmills.com

Bob's Red Mill (especially almond meal/flour and wheat gluten)
Bob's Red Mill Natural Foods
www.bobsredmill.com

King Arthur Flours (especially whole wheat and white whole wheat)
King Arthur Flour Co.
www.kingarthurflour.com

Candies and chocolate

Asher's sugar-free product line
Asher's Chocolates Inc.
www.ashers.com

Repertoire sugar-free chocolate line (milk, dark, and bittersweet)
Dorval Trading Co., Ltd.
www.dorvaltrading.com (buy them at natural foods stores, etc.)

Russel Stover low-carb product line
Russell Stover Candies, Inc.
www.russellstover.com

La Nouba sugar-free marshmallows
La Nouba
www.lanouba.be

Cookies

Murray sugar-free product line
Murray Biscuit Co., LLC (find them at your supermarket)

Convenience mixes (cake, brownie, muffin, pudding)

Atkins product line (especially brownie mix, muffin mix and "Bake Mix")
Atkins Nutritionals, Inc.
www.atkins.com

Jell-O sugar-free, fat-free pudding mixes, and sugar-free gelatin mixes
Kraft Foods North America, Inc.
www.jello.com

Sweet'N Low no-sugar-added cake and frosting mixes
Bernard Food Industries, Inc.
www.edietshop.com

CarbSense product line (especially granola, baking mixes)
CarbSense Foods
www.carbsense.com

Sweeteners

Splenda
McNeil Nutritionals
www.splenda.com

Sugar Twin brown sugar substitute
Alberto-Culver USA, Inc.
www.sugartwin.com

Miscellaneous

Expert Foods product line (including ThickenThin thickener products,
    Cake-ability, etc.)
Expert Foods, Inc.
www.expertfoods.com

Smucker's sugar-free "light" preserves
J. M. Smucker Co.
www.smuckers.com

Atkins sugar-free syrups
Atkins Nutritionals, Inc.
www.atkins.com

low-carb dessert tips and techniques

THIS IS A collection of hints that I used when developing the recipes for this book. They're divided into sections by topic to make it easier for you to find the information you're seeking.

Ingredients in General

- High-quality ingredients make for high-quality desserts; it's that simple. Buying the best fresh berries you can find, the best low-carb bread you can find (as long as it meets your carb limitations), and the best low-carb ice cream available in your area, for example, will all go a long way toward making your desserts exceptionally good.

- In cases where I've specified a brand, it's because I've found that brand to work the best in these recipes. It does not mean you need to also use that brand, or that the recipe won't turn out okay if you don't use that brand—it's just a recommendation.

- Locating low-carb ingredients gets easier every day, as more and more products become available, and as regular supermarkets begin to carry more low-carb items. I usually recommend also looking for ingredients at health food stores, natural foods stores, and even at mass-market retailers and discount stores. If you don't see the item you need, don't be afraid to ask a clerk for assistance; many times they'll order special products if they know you'll be buying them regularly (I got my grocery store to carry unsweetened organic coconut this way). Also, check out online sources for ingredients, especially if you live in an area where there aren't many stores that carry low-carb foods.

- Before beginning to cook, assemble all the necessary ingredients on the counter, as well as all the tools (whisks, measuring spoons, etc.) you'll need. It saves you time in the long run and can help you avoid the dreaded forgotten-ingredient syndrome.

Specific Ingredients

ALMOND MEAL/FLOUR: I like to purchase this product, rather than grind up my own almonds, because the packaged product is much finer in texture than what I can usually achieve at home with my food processor or coffee grinder. However, in a pinch, I do make my own almond meal. To make your own almond meal at home, start with blanched, slivered almonds (not whole almonds or sliced almonds). Process them in a small food chopper, food processor, or clean coffee grinder until they are very finely chopped, or ground. Overprocessing them will turn them into almond butter, so do keep an eye on them, and stop to check the progress frequently during processing. Store almond meal (whether packaged or homemade) in a plastic container or zip-top plastic bag, in the refrigerator, in order to avoid rapid spoilage.

BUTTER: Unless otherwise specified, I've used regular salted butter in these recipes. If you opt to use margarine instead, make sure to use stick margarine, not whipped "light" or soft tub margarine. The higher water content of these margarines can ruin the texture of some desserts. Some recipes call for cold butter, which is then diced (such as for the Low-Carb Fruit Crisp Topping on page 204). An easy way to ensure that you always have some really cold butter when you need it is to keep one stick of butter in the freezer. You can grate it on the coarse side of a hand grater, using the markings on the butter wrapper as a guide. Or, when you're reading through the recipe before you begin to cook, simply put the amount of butter you need in the freezer; by the time you're ready for it, it will be cold and ready to dice with a sharp paring knife.

EGGS: All the recipes in this book were developed using large eggs, which is the standard for baking purposes. In certain recipes, such as meringues, where the texture of the product is greatly (or exclusively) dependent on whipped egg whites, it's wise to use room-temperature eggs. Eggs that are taken right from the refrigerator and then whipped will not achieve as great a volume as room-temperature eggs. Bring eggs to room temperature by leaving them on the counter for about 20 to 30 minutes (and not longer than 45 minutes, for food safety reasons).

WHIPPING CREAM: You can use either heavy cream or cream that's labeled "whipping cream"—either will work. The important thing to remember is that the cream needs to be very cold in order to whip up light and fluffy. Cream that is at room temperature does not achieve optimal volume. Although in general I recommend collecting all your ingredients before beginning to cook, I make an exception in the case of whipping cream: leave it in the refrigerator until you're ready to whip it. Even better, chill your mixing bowl, too, if you can! Whipped cream that's kept for a day or two in the refrigerator is perfectly good to eat, but it usually loses some of its volume and is no longer fluffy. To revive it, simple whisk it quickly by hand for a minute or two.

• TIMING ISSUES •

- You'll notice that all of the recipes give estimated preparation times, as well as cooking times. Before planning which dessert to make, check those timing estimates. Unless you want the dessert to be served warm, in most cases you'll need to begin making desserts early in the day in order to have time for them to bake, set, cool, or chill.

- If you're cooking with an electric range/oven, you may need to increase the cooking times slightly. The recipes in this book were developed using a gas range/oven. Regardless of whether you have a gas or electric appliance, all of the recipes in this book can be prepared in any kitchen with standard appliances.

- Desserts that are to be served warm can sometimes be a challenge for cooks who also have a dinner to prepare. In many cases, these desserts, such as the Milk Chocolate–Almond Souffle for Two on page 118, can be put into the oven when you sit down for dinner; they'll be ready just about when you're ready for dessert. Again, be sure to check the timing estimates indicated with the recipes, and set your timers so you don't forget about the dessert in the oven!

- For baking, shiny metal pans are preferred, as they reflect heat away from the product and produce a light brown crust. Dark, nonstick metal pans and cookie sheets, and glass pans all absorb heat, so desserts baked in these pans will bake and brown faster. Keep this in mind when setting your timer.

- It's usually recommended that when baking a pie crust or pie in a glass or ceramic pie plate (as opposed to a metal one), you'll need to decrease the baking temperature by 25°F, and check for doneness earlier than specified in the recipe.

- Save time in your kitchen by organizing and locating the pots, pans, and tools that you use frequently in easily accessible cabinets and drawers. It seems obvious, but many people organize their kitchens not for practical use, but by another method that ends up not being very useful. I also organize my spices, keeping them not in alphabetical order, but by putting the ones I use most frequently in front where I can see them and reach them quickly; the ones I use less frequently go in back or up higher.

- Cheesecakes are a great make-ahead "company's coming" dessert. Most cheesecakes benefit from chilling overnight in the refrigerator; you'll have an easier time cutting them, and their texture is best when they've had plenty of time to chill. All cheesecakes can be prepared one day ahead of time, then covered and refrigerated.

• TECHNIQUES •

Blending Sweeteners

In some recipes you'll see that I've used a combination of Splenda Granular (my preferred sweetener) and a small amount of real sugar. Although most low-carbers shun sugar in any form, I've found that by using just a small amount of it, along with another sweetener, greatly improves the final product in two major ways. First, this technique helps eliminate the "fake" sweetener taste that can occur when you use just Splenda (or some other artifical sweetener) with little or no impact on the net carb content per serving.

The second reason I do this is for "food science" reasons, such as texture and browning. Certain baked goods that are made solely with sweeteners don't brown as readily as those made with real sugar. In some instances this is fine, but in others, a nice browning is desirable for a dessert. Sugar also affects the texture of products, contributing especially to their moistness. I've tested these recipes numerous times and found that the sugar–sweetener combination technique works well. Whether you choose to use real sugar in your low-carb dessert recipes is up to you. However, if you opt to use no real sugar at all (and use only Splenda or another sweetener), be aware that the results may be adversely affected.

Grating citrus peel

Lemon, lime, and orange peel bring a shot of intense fresh flavor to many desserts, without adding carbs or calories. Grated citrus peel, also known as zest, is also a suitable garnish for fruit desserts. When grating citrus, it's important to remove only the colored, outer layer of the peel, not the white pith below, which is bitter. To properly grate citrus, first wash and scrub the fruit, and dry it. Use the fine side of a hand grater, or invest in a microplane grater (a long metal grater designed specifically for zesting fruit), and turn the fruit after each pass over the grater, in order to only get the outside layer. If you don't have an appropriate grater, you can use a very sharp paring knife instead. Cut off only the very outer layer of the peel, and then finely mince it.

Inverting cakes

Inverting a cake from its baking pan simply means turning it upside down to remove it from the pan. First, let the cake cool at least 10 minutes before inverting (unless the recipe specifies otherwise). Then, run a butter knife around the inside edge of the pan to loosen the cake. Place a clean kitchen towel or piece of waxed paper on top of the cake, then place a wire cooling rack (or a plate) over the waxed paper, on top of the cake. Using a smooth yet rapid motion, turn both the rack and pan upside down together, flipping the cake onto the rack; lift off the cake pan. If you like, you can then flip the cake back over onto a serving plate or second wire rack, then remove the waxed paper or kitchen towel. Let cake cool completely on the wire rack or plate.

Toasting nuts and coconut

Toasted nuts are known to have more flavor than untoasted nuts. Some of these recipes call for toasted nuts, and others don't—it's always your option to toast them if you'd like. Toasted coconut is frequently used as a garnish for desserts. To toast either nuts or coconut, spread a single layer of nuts or coconut on a baking sheet with a rim. Bake in the center of a preheated 350°F oven for about 5 minutes. Do *not* walk away; you need to be in the kitchen where you can keep an eye on the progress, as both nuts and coconut can go from perfectly toasted to completely burned *very* quickly.

• USING SOME HIGHER-CARB, OR "REAL" INGREDIENTS •

I DON'T DO it in every recipe, but in some recipes, this technique makes a huge difference in the quality of the finished dessert. Basically, the premise is the same as that for using a little real sugar along with a sweetener. By using a little all-purpose flour or flavored liqueur (as opposed to just a flavoring), the dessert is improved—and with little or no impact on net carbs. The trick here is to keep the amount of the "real" ingredient small, not to overdo it. Again, if you've already decided that a dessert can be part of your eating plan, and you keep your portions in control, then the tiny amounts of real sugar or flour in these recipes won't be enough to damage your low-carb regimen.

cakes and cheesecakes

boston cream pie

• •

ESTIMATED PREPARATION TIME: 15 minutes (plus at least 1 hour cooling time)
COOK TIME: 25 minutes • **SERVINGS:** 10

• •

THIS MISNAMED CLASSIC (it's really a cake, not a pie) gets a low-carb makeover—without losing any of its appeal. A creamy, vanilla filling is sandwiched between layers of yellow cake, and it's all topped with rich Chocolate Glaze. If you'd rather not have leftover dry pudding mix, stir it into about 1 cup of low-carb milk for a snack later.

for the cake layers:
cooking spray
¾ cup cold water
½ teaspoon vanilla extract
1 8-ounce package Sweet'N Low no-added-sugar yellow cake mix

for the vanilla cream:
1½ cups whipping cream
2 tablespoons plus ½ teaspoon sugar-free, fat-free instant vanilla pudding mix

1 recipe Chocolate Glaze (page 198)

1. Preheat the oven to 375°F. Spray an 8-inch round cake pan with cooking spray; set aside.
2. *To make the cake:* In a 1-cup measuring cup for liquids, stir together the water and vanilla. Add the cake mix to a medium mixing bowl, then add half the water mixture; mix with an electric mixer on low speed for 1 minute. Scrape the bowl with a rubber spatula, then increase mixer speed to medium and mix for another minute. Scrape bowl again, add remaining water mixture, and mix on medium-high speed another 2 minutes, until well blended.
3. Pour batter into prepared cake pan. Bake for 25 minutes, or until cake springs back when touched lightly in the center. Remove from the oven and let cool completely, about 1 hour. While cake is cooling, prepare the vanilla cream filling.
4. *To make the vanilla cream:* In a medium mixing bowl, using an electric mixer, whip ingredients together on medium-high speed for about 2 minutes, scraping bowl occasionally, until mixture is fluffy.

5. Remove the cooled cake from the pan and split it in half horizontally using a serrated knife.

6. Using a rubber spatula, spread the vanilla cream filling over the bottom layer, almost to the edges. Top with the second layer, pressing it down gently with your hands to squeeze the filling to the edge of the cake. Pour the Chocolate Glaze over the top of the cake. Use a rubber spatula to smooth it just to the edges (it should not run down the sides). Refrigerate until serving time.

---

cook's tip

If the glaze doesn't seem thick enough to use immediately, chill it briefly in the refrigerator to thicken before pouring it over the cake.

• **APPROXIMATE NUTRITIONAL CONTENT** •
Calories: 254, Protein: 3g, Net Carbs: 12g, Fat: 19g, Cholesterol: 53mg, Sodium: 94mg

mocha cream torte

● ●

ESTIMATED PREPARATION TIME: 10 minutes (plus at least 1 hour cooling time)
COOK TIME: 25 minutes • **SERVINGS:** 10

● ●

THIS DECADENT TORTE features two chocolate cake layers flavored with brewed coffee, a generous amount of fluffy mocha filling, and a decadent chocolate glaze. I found while testing this that I prefer a dark chocolate glaze, so I used sugar-free dark chocolate, but feel free to use your favorite type or combination of chocolates.

●

for the cake layers:
cooking spray
¾ cup cold brewed coffee, divided
1 8-ounce package Sweet'N Low no-added-sugar chocolate cake mix

for the mocha cream:
1½ cups whipping cream
2 tablespoons instant coffee crystals
2 tablespoons plus ½ teaspoon sugar-free, fat-free instant chocolate pudding mix

1 recipe Chocolate Glaze (page 198)

●

1. Preheat the oven to 375°F. Spray an 8-inch round cake pan with cooking spray; set aside.
2. *To make the cake:* In a medium mixing bowl, using an electric mixer on low speed, mix half the cold coffee with the chocolate cake mix for 2 minutes. Scrape the bowl with a rubber spatula, then increase mixer speed to medium and mix another minute. Scrape bowl again, add remaining coffee, and mix on medium speed another 2 minutes, until well blended. Pour batter into prepared cake pan.
3. Bake for 25 minutes, or until cake springs back when touched lightly in the center. Remove from the oven and let cool completely, about 1 hour. While cake is cooling, prepare the mocha cream.
4. *To make the mocha cream:* In a 2-cup measuring cup for liquids, stir together the whipping cream and instant coffee crystals until the coffee is dissolved. Pour the cream mixture into a medium mixing bowl and add the pudding mix. Using an electric mixer, whip ingredients together on medium-high speed about 2 minutes, scraping bowl occasionally, until mixture is fluffy.

5. Remove the cooled cake from the pan and split the cake in half horizontally using a serrated knife.

6. Using a rubber spatula, spread the mocha cream over the bottom layer, almost to the edges. Top with the second layer, pressing it down gently with your hands to squeeze the filling to the edge of the cake. Pour the Chocolate Glaze over the top of the cake. Use a rubber spatula to smooth it just to the edges (it should not run down the sides). Refrigerate until serving time.

cook's Tip

If the glaze seems too thin to use immediately, chill it briefly in the refrigerator to thicken it before spreading it on the cake.

• APPROXIMATE NUTRITIONAL CONTENT •

Calories: 258, Protein: 3g, Net Carbs: 13g, Fat: 19g, Cholesterol: 53mg, Sodium: 95mg

frosted coconut cake

ESTIMATED PREPARATION TIME: 10 minutes (plus at least 2 hours cooling time)
COOK TIME: 25 minutes • SERVINGS: 10

THIS ONE-LAYER cake contains many coconut ingredients—coconut milk, coconut extract, and unsweetened coconut. The combination results in a rich coconut flavor throughout both the cake and the frosting. Be sure to refrigerate any leftover cake.

for the cake:
cooking spray

¾ cup water

¼ cup unsweetened coconut milk

2 tablespoons unsweetened coconut

1 tablespoon Splenda Granular sweetener

1½ teaspoons coconut extract

1 8-ounce package Sweet'N Low no-added-sugar white or yellow cake mix

for the frosting:
¼ cup whipping cream

4 ounces cream cheese, softened

2 tablespoons cold water

1½ teaspoons coconut extract

¼ teaspoon vanilla extract

½ cup Sweet'N Low no-added-sugar white frosting mix

¼ cup unsweetened coconut

1 tablespoon unsweetened coconut, toasted, for garnish

1. Preheat the oven to 375°F. Spray an 8-inch round cake pan with cooking spray; set aside.

2. *To make the cake:* In a medium mixing bowl, combine the water, coconut milk, coconut, Splenda, and extracts. Using an electric mixer on low speed, mix about 1 minute, until blended, scraping bowl with a rubber spatula once during mixing. Add the cake mix and blend on low speed, gradually increasing to medium-high speed, until well mixed, about 4 minutes. Pour the batter into the prepared pan.

3. Bake for 25 minutes, or until top is golden brown and springs back when touched lightly in the center. Remove from the oven and let cool completely, about 2 hours. While cake is cooling, prepare the frosting.

4. *To make the frosting:* In a small mixing bowl, using an electric mixer on medium speed, mix the whipping cream and cream cheese until blended and smooth. Add the cold water, extracts, and frosting mix and blend on low speed, gradually increasing to medium-high speed, until frosting is smooth, about 5 minutes. Add the ¼ cup coconut and mix for 1 minute to combine.

5. Remove the cooled cake from the pan. Using a butter knife or small rubber spatula, spread the frosting on the cooled cake, covering the sides and top. Sprinkle the top with the toasted coconut to garnish.

• **APPROXIMATE NUTRITIONAL CONTENT** •
Calories: 156, Protein: 2g, Net Carbs: 11g, Fat: 8g, Cholesterol: 8mg, Sodium: 27mg

flourless chocolate cake

ESTIMATED PREPARATION TIME: 20 minutes (plus 15–30 minutes cooling time)
COOK TIME: 30 minutes • **SERVINGS:** 8

RICH, DECADENT CHOCOLATE cake is on almost everyone's list of all-time favorite recipes. Luckily, because it's flourless, it's remarkably easy to convert to a low-carb recipe. Before my low-carb days, this used to be one of my signature recipes, and now this version reigns at our house (guests don't even know the difference)! I think it's best served slightly warm (put it in to bake when you sit down for dinner) with fresh raspberries and plenty of Homemade Whipped Cream.

cooking spray
8 tablespoons butter, softened, divided
2 3-ounce bars sugar-free bittersweet chocolate, chopped
2 3-ounce bars sugar-free dark chocolate, chopped
½ teaspoon vanilla extract
⅛ teaspoon instant coffee crystals
5 eggs, room temperature
2 tablespoons sugar
⅛ teaspoon salt
2 cups Homemade Whipped Cream (page 190)
Fresh raspberries, optional

1. Preheat the oven to 350°F. Lightly spray the bottom of an 8-inch springform pan with cooking spray. Cut a piece of waxed paper or parchment paper, to fit the bottom and line the pan with it (the cooking spray helps it stick). Use 1 table-spoon of the butter to grease the top of the waxed paper and sides of the pan well; set aside.

2. In a heavy, medium saucepan, melt the remaining butter and the chocolate over low heat, stirring occasionally with a wooden spoon. When smooth and blended, remove from heat and stir in the vanilla extract and instant coffee until smooth and blended; set aside.

3. In a medium mixing bowl, using an electric mixer on medium speed, mix the eggs, sugar, and salt for 5 minutes, or until thick and tripled in volume. Whisk about one-quarter of the egg mixture into the reserved chocolate mixture. Then,

using a rubber spatula, gently stir the chocolate mixture into the mixing bowl with the remaining egg mixture until just blended (do not overmix).

4. Transfer the batter to the prepared pan. Bake 30 minutes, until the sides are set but the center still jiggles slightly when the pan is gently shaken.

5. Remove from the oven and let cool 15 minutes in the pan. Run a knife around the inside edge of the pan to loosen the cake; remove the ring. Using a long knife, cut the cake into 8 servings. Serve warm, if possible, with Homemade Whipped Cream and raspberries, if desired.

cook's tip

If the cake cools too long, the consistency changes: it gets quite firm. This is easily remedied by microwaving individual portions on MEDIUM power for about 15 seconds.

• APPROXIMATE NUTRITIONAL CONTENT •
Calories: 335, Protein: 7g, Net Carbs: 3g, Fat: 29g, Cholesterol: 164mg, Sodium: 195mg

almond roulade with raspberry cream filling

* *

ESTIMATED PREPARATION TIME: 15 minutes (plus at least 2½ hours cooling/chilling time)
COOK TIME: 12 minutes • **SERVINGS:** 10

* *

THIS IS A party-perfect cake—pretty, delicious, and completely make-ahead. For an extra-special presentation, serve each slice atop a pool of Raspberry Coulis.

for the cake roll:
cooking spray
1 tablespoon all-purpose flour
5 eggs, separated
1 teaspoon almond extract
½ teaspoon vanilla extract
½ teaspoon salt
⅓ cup Splenda Granular sweetener
2 tablespoons light brown sugar
¼ cup cornstarch
1 teaspoon baking powder
¾ cup almond meal/flour (or very finely chopped almonds), divided

for the raspberry cream filling:
1 8-ounce package cream cheese, softened
2 tablespoons fresh lemon juice
2 tablespoons sugar-free "light" raspberry preserves (such as Smucker's)
1 half-pint container fresh raspberries, washed and air-dried (about 1 cup)
¼ cup light cream
½ cup Splenda Granular sweetener

1 recipe Raspberry Coulis (optional) (page 201)

1. Preheat the oven to 375°F. Lightly coat a 10½-by-15½-inch jelly roll pan with cooking spray. Cover the pan with parchment paper or waxed paper (the cooking spray helps it stick). Heavily coat the parchment paper with cooking spray, then dust the paper with the flour.

2. *To make the cake roll:* In a small bowl, stir together the egg yolks and the extracts; set aside. In a medium mixing bowl, using an electric mixer on high speed, beat the egg whites until foamy. Add the salt and beat again until the eggs form soft peaks. Turn the mixer speed down to medium and mix in the Splenda and brown sugar; turn the mixer speed back up to high and continue to beat until mixture is stiff, but not dry.

3. Pour the reserved yolk mixture over the egg white mixture and sprinkle with the cornstarch, baking powder, and ½ cup of the almond meal. Using a wooden spoon, gently stir until all ingredients are blended (do not overmix or the egg whites will deflate). Spread the batter in the prepared pan, smoothing the top with a rubber spatula. Bake cake for 12 minutes, or until cake springs back when touched lightly in the center, and surface is lightly browned.

4. While cake is baking, spread a clean kitchen towel or tea towel on the counter. Sprinkle the towel with the remaining ¼ cup of almond meal; using clean hands, spread the nuts evenly over the towel. When cake is done baking, remove it from the oven and immediately invert it onto the prepared towel. Carefully peel off the parchment paper and use a sharp knife to trim any crisp or uneven edges.

5. Gently roll the cake up in the towel, starting from a long edge (the towel will be rolled up inside the cake—that's okay!). Let the cake rest, rolled up in the towel, for 3 minutes, then unroll it and let it rest about 3 minutes more. Roll it up again (with the towel) and let the cake cool completely, about ½ hour. While waiting for the cake to cool, prepare the cream filling.

6. *To make the filling:* In a medium mixing bowl, using an electric mixer on medium speed, mix the cream cheese, lemon juice, and preserves until smooth. Add the light cream and Splenda, and mix again until blended. Using a wooden spoon, stir the raspberries into the cream mixture.

7. When cake is cool, unroll it. Using a rubber spatula, spread the cream filling over the inside, leaving a ½-inch border clear of filling all around the edge (this helps keep the filling from leaking out when you roll it back up). Roll the cake up again (this time without the towel inside), and carefully place the roll on a platter. Refrigerate the roll for at least 2 hours, lightly covered with plastic wrap.

8. To serve, use a serrated knife and cut the roll into 10 equal slices. If serving with Raspberry Coulis, use about 3 tablespoons per portion and spread the coulis into a circle on individual dessert plates so that when the roulade is placed on top, the coulis still shows from underneath.

• **APPROXIMATE NUTRITIONAL CONTENT** •
Calories: 204, Protein: 7g, Net Carbs: 9g, Fat: 16g, Cholesterol: 135mg, Sodium: 257mg

banana-toffee snack cake

ESTIMATED PREPARATION TIME: 15 minutes (plus at least 2 hours cooling time)
COOK TIME: 30 minutes • **SERVINGS:** 20

THIS EASY RECIPE starts with a muffin mix, to which you add some mashed banana, extra nuts, and a little vanilla. Topped with a generous amount of rich cream cheese frosting and crunchy toffee pieces, it's a snack cake that'll please both adults and kids.

for the cake:
cooking spray
1 8-ounce package Atkins Quick Quisine Banana Nut Muffin Mix
1/2 cup vegetable oil
1 cup water
2 eggs, lightly beaten
1 small ripe banana, mashed (about 1/2 cup)
1/4 cup walnuts or pecans, finely chopped
1/2 teaspoon vanilla extract

for the frosting:
2 recipes Cream Cheese Frosting (page 196)
1 1-ounce sugar-free toffee bar, crushed

1. Preheat the oven to 350°F. Spray a 13-by-9-inch baking pan with cooking spray; set aside.

2. *To make the cake:* In a large mixing bowl, using a wooden spoon, stir together all the cake ingredients until just combined (do not overmix!). Using a rubber spatula, spread the batter into the prepared pan, smoothing the top.

3. Bake for 30 minutes, until lightly browned. Remove from the oven and let cool completely, about 2 hours. While cake is cooling, prepare the Cream Cheese Frosting.

4. Frost the cake using a rubber spatula, spreading the frosting smooth. Sprinkle the top with the crushed toffee. Cut cake into 20 squares. Refrigerate until serving time.

• APPROXIMATE NUTRITIONAL CONTENT •
Calories: 192, Protein: 6g, Net Carbs: 3g, Fat: 16g, Cholesterol: 44mg, Sodium: 149mg

black forest cupcakes

ESTIMATED PREPARATION TIME: 10 minutes (plus at least $^1/_2$ hour cooling time)
COOK TIME: 20 minutes • **SERVINGS:** 10

THESE CUPCAKES are a bit more special than a regular cupcake, but not at all challenging to prepare. Be sure to purchase the no-added-sugar pie filling, rather than the "light" version, which is still quite high in carbs.

$^2/_3$ cup water
2 tablespoons Atkins Sugar-Free Chocolate Syrup
$^1/_2$ teaspoon vanilla extract
1 8-ounce package Sweet'N Low no-added-sugar chocolate cake mix
1 tablespoon unsweetened cocoa powder
$^2/_3$ cup no-added-sugar cherry pie filling (not "light" pie filling)
2 ounces sugar-free milk chocolate, chopped

1. Preheat the oven to 375°F. Line a muffin tin with cupcake liners; set aside.
2. In a measuring cup for liquids, stir together the water, chocolate syrup, and vanilla. Pour the mixture into a medium mixing bowl. Add the chocolate cake mix and cocoa to the bowl.
3. Using an electric mixer on low speed, mix the ingredients until combined, then increase the speed to medium-high and beat until smooth and almost fluffy, about 4 minutes, scraping bowl occasionally.
4. Using a tablespoon measure, place one scoop of batter into the bottom of each liner. Using a teaspoon measure, place a generous scoop of cherry pie filling on top of the batter, centering it as best you can (you should get 2 to 3 cherries in each portion). Top the cherry filling with another scant tablespoon of batter (it's okay if it doesn't completely cover the cherry pie filling, because it will spread when it bakes). Sprinkle chopped chocolate over the top of each cupcake.
5. Bake for 20 minutes, or until the top springs back when lightly touched; remove from oven and let cool for 5 minutes. Remove the cupcakes from the pan and let them cool at least another 25 minutes before serving.

• **APPROXIMATE NUTRITIONAL CONTENT** •
Calories: 119, Protein: 2g, Net Carbs: 13.5g, Fat: 3g, Cholesterol: 0mg, Sodium: 22mg

coconut "joy" cheesecake

ESTIMATED PREPARATION TIME: 15 minutes (plus at least 5 hours cooling/chilling time)
COOK TIME: 50 minutes • **SERVINGS:** 8

*L*IKE THE CANDY bar after which it's named, this cheesecake features the fabulous flavor combination of coconut, chocolate, and crunchy almonds.

for the crust:
cooking spray
1 recipe Chocolate Graham Crust (page 62)

for the cheese filling:
1 8-ounce package cream cheese, softened
1 8-ounce package Neufchâtel cheese, softened
2 eggs
$\frac{1}{4}$ cup whipping cream
$\frac{1}{2}$ cup plus 1 tablespoon Splenda Granular sweetener
$\frac{1}{3}$ cup unsweetened coconut milk
$1\frac{1}{4}$ teaspoons coconut extract
$\frac{1}{4}$ cup unsweetened coconut

1 recipe Chocolate Glaze (page 198)

1. Preheat the oven to 350°F.
2. *To make the crust:* Spray the bottom and sides of an 8-inch springform pan with cooking spray. Press the Chocolate Graham Crust mixture onto the bottom and slightly up the sides of the pan. Bake crust 8 minutes; remove from oven to cool, but leave oven on. While crust is cooling, prepare the cheese filling.
3. *To make the filling:* In a large mixing bowl, using an electric mixer on medium speed, mix together the softened cheeses and the eggs, scraping bowl occasionally, until smooth. Add all remaining ingredients, except for the Chocolate Glaze, and mix until very smooth and almost fluffy, about 5 minutes.
4. Pour filling into cooled crust. Cover the top of the pan with foil, tenting it slightly in the middle so the cake doesn't touch the foil when it rises during baking, and bake for 50 minutes.

5. Remove cake from oven, lift off foil, and run a sharp knife around the inside edge of the pan to loosen cake. Let the cake cool 1 hour, then refrigerate for 3 hours. Toward the end of the cake's chilling time, prepare the Chocolate Glaze.

6. After cake has chilled, remove the ring from around the pan. Using a rubber spatula, spread the glaze smoothly over the top of the cake, filling the depression in the middle of the cake (the glaze should not reach the edges). Return cake to the refrigerator for 1 more hour before serving.

• **APPROXIMATE NUTRITIONAL CONTENT** •

Calories: 457, Protein: 11g, Net Carbs: 8.5g, Fat: 41g, Cholesterol: 137mg, Sodium: 304mg

new york—style cheesecake

ESTIMATED PREPARATION TIME: 15 minutes (plus at least 6 hours cooling/chilling time)
COOK TIME: 1 hour and 15 minutes • **SERVINGS:** 10

....

$\mathcal{C}$LASSIC NEW YORK cheesecake is rich, creamy, and has a hint of lemon—perfect for topping any way you like. Try fresh fruit or one of the toppings from the "Extras" chapter (pages 189 to 205).

for the crust:
cooking spray
5 large graham cracker rectangles, crushed (about ¾ cup crumbs)
2 tablespoons butter, melted

for the cheese filling:
2 8-ounce packages Neufchâtel cheese, softened
1 8-ounce package cream cheese, softened
3 eggs
¼ cup whipping cream
½ cup sour cream (not "light" or fat-free)
⅔ cup Splenda Granular sweetener
1 teaspoon vanilla extract
1 tablespoon grated lemon peel

1. Preheat the oven to 350°F.

2. *To make the crust:* Spray the bottom and sides of an 8-inch springform pan with cooking spray. In a small bowl, combine the graham cracker crumbs with the melted butter. Pat the mixture into the bottom of the pan, forming an even, but thin crust. Bake crust 8 minutes; remove from oven to cool, but leave oven on. While crust is cooling, prepare cheese filling.

3. *To make the filling:* In a large mixing bowl, using an electric mixer on medium speed, blend together the softened cheeses and the eggs, scraping bowl occasionally, until smooth. Add all remaining ingredients and mix until very smooth and almost fluffy, about 5 minutes.

4. Pour filling into cooled crust. Cover the top of the pan with foil, tenting it slightly in the middle so the cake doesn't touch the foil when it rises during baking.

everyday low-carb desserts
34

5. Bake for 1 hour, then turn off the oven and let the cake sit in the closed oven for 15 minutes more. Remove cake from oven, lift off foil, and run a sharp knife around the inside edge of the pan to loosen cake. Let the cake cool 1 hour; then remove the ring from around the pan. Refrigerate for 5 hours before serving.

• **APPROXIMATE NUTRITIONAL CONTENT** •
Calories: 324, Protein: 9g, Net Carbs: 9.5g, Fat: 28g, Cholesterol: 143mg, Sodium: 353mg

"turtle" cheesecake

ESTIMATED PREPARATION TIME: 15 minutes (plus at least 4 hours cooling/chilling time)
COOK TIME: 45 minutes • **SERVINGS:** 10

REMINISCENT OF THOSE delicious candies called "turtles," this cheesecake boasts a nutty crust and a decadent chocolate-pecan topping.

for the crust:
cooking spray
1 recipe Nutty Graham Crust, made with pecans (page 61)

for the cheese filling:
1 8-ounce package Neufchâtel cheese, softened
2 8-ounce packages cream cheese, softened
3 eggs
½ cup whipping cream
¾ cup Splenda Granular sweetener
2 teaspoons vanilla extract
¼ cup pecans, toasted and chopped
1 ounce sugar-free dark chocolate, coarsely chopped

for the topping:
6 Russell Stover Sugar-Free Pecan Delights, chopped
1 ounce sugar-free milk chocolate, chopped

1. Preheat the oven to 350°F.
2. *To make the crust:* Spray the bottom and sides of a 9-inch springform pan with cooking spray. Press the Nutty Graham Crust mixture onto the bottom of the pan. Bake crust 8 minutes; remove from oven to cool, but leave oven on. While crust is cooling, prepare cheese filling.
3. *To make the filling:* In a large mixing bowl, using an electric mixer on medium speed, blend together the softened cheeses and the eggs, scraping bowl occasionally, until smooth. Add all remaining filling ingredients and mix until almost fluffy, about 5 minutes.

4. Pour filling into crust. Cover the top of the pan with foil, tenting it slightly in the middle so the cake doesn't touch the foil when it rises during baking, and bake for 45 minutes.

5. Remove cake from oven, lift off foil, and run a sharp knife around the inside edge of the pan to loosen cake. Sprinkle the top of the cake with the topping ingredients; let cake cool 1 hour. Remove the ring from around the pan, then refrigerate for 3 hours before serving.

• **APPROXIMATE NUTRITIONAL CONTENT** •
Calories: 498, Protein: 10g, Net Carbs: 12g, Fat: 46g, Cholesterol: 160mg, Sodium: 361mg

triple-chocolate cheesecake

ESTIMATED PREPARATION TIME: 15 minutes (plus 5 hours cooling/chilling time)
COOK TIME: 50 minutes • **SERVINGS:** 12

A CHOCOLATE GRAHAM crust, plus a rich, creamy chocolate cheese filling and smooth chocolate glaze makes this cake a chocoholic's dream dessert.

for the crust:
cooking spray
1 recipe Chocolate Graham Crust (page 62)

for the cheese filling:
1 8-ounce package Neufchâtel cheese, softened
2 8-ounce packages cream cheese, softened
⅓ cup sour cream (not fat-free or "light")
3 eggs
¼ cup whipping cream
2 tablespoons low-carb chocolate syrup
1 teaspoon instant coffee crystals
1 teaspoon vanilla extract
pinch of salt
2 3-ounce bars sugar-free bittersweet chocolate, chopped
⅔ cup Splenda Granular sweetener

1 recipe Chocolate Glaze (page 198)

1. Preheat the oven to 350°F.
2. *To make the crust:* Spray the bottom and sides of a 9-inch springform pan with cooking spray. Press the Chocolate Graham Crust mixture onto the bottom of the pan. Bake crust 8 minutes; remove from oven to cool, but leave oven on. While crust is cooling, prepare cheese filling.
3. *To make the filling:* In a large mixing bowl, using an electric mixer on medium speed, blend together the softened cheeses, sour cream, and the eggs, scraping bowl occasionally, until smooth.
4. In a microwavable bowl, stir together the whipping cream, chocolate syrup, instant coffee, vanilla, and salt. Microwave mixture on LOW power for 1 to 2 min-

utes, until just simmering, then stir in the chopped chocolate until melted and smooth. Add the chocolate mixture to the mixing bowl with the cream cheese mixture; stir for 1 minute to combine. Add the Splenda and mix on medium speed about 3 minutes, scraping bowl occasionally, until blended.

5. Pour filling into cooled crust. Bake 50 minutes (it will still jiggle in the center when the pan is gently shaken). Remove cake from oven and run a sharp knife around the inside edge of the pan to loosen cake. Let the cake cool 1 hour, then refrigerate for 3 hours. Toward the end of the cake's chilling time, prepare the Chocolate Glaze.

6. After cake has chilled, remove the ring from around the pan. Using a rubber spatula, spread the glaze smoothly over the top of the cake, filling the depression in the middle of the cake (the glaze should not reach the edges). Return cake to the refrigerator for 1 more hour before serving.

• APPROXIMATE NUTRITIONAL CONTENT •
Calories: 430, Protein: 10g, Net Carbs: 7g, Fat: 39g, Cholesterol: 134mg, Sodium: 283mg

peanut butter cup cheesecake

ESTIMATED PREPARATION TIME: 15 minutes (plus at least 5 hours cooling/chilling time)
COOK TIME: 1 hour • SERVINGS: 12

THE "CAN'T MISS" combination of peanut butter and chocolate makes a successful and popular cheesecake. You'll note that the crust recipe makes more crust than used on the other cheesecakes; that's because this cheesecake works better if the crust extends up the sides of the pan a little, so you need more crust mixture.

for the crust:

cooking spray
7 chocolate graham crackers, crushed (about 1 cup crumbs)
¼ cup "cocktail" peanuts, finely chopped
4 tablespoons butter, melted

for the cheese filling:

1 8-ounce package Neufchâtel cheese, softened
2 8-ounce packages cream cheese, softened
¾ cup low-carb peanut butter
3 eggs
½ cup whipping cream
1 cup Splenda Granular sweetener
1 teaspoon vanilla extract

1 recipe Chocolate Glaze (page 198)

1. Preheat the oven to 350°F.
2. *To make the crust:* Spray the bottom and sides of a 9-inch springform pan with cooking spray. In a small bowl, combine the graham cracker crumbs with the chopped peanuts and melted butter. Pat mixture into the bottom and about ½ inch up the sides of the pan. Bake crust 8 minutes; remove from oven to cool, but leave oven on. While crust is cooling, prepare cheese filling.
3. *To make the filling:* In a large mixing bowl, using an electric mixer on medium speed, blend together the softened cheeses, peanut butter, and eggs, scraping bowl occasionally, until smooth. Add all remaining filling ingredients and mix until almost fluffy, about 5 minutes.

4. Pour filling into cooled crust. Cover the top of the pan with foil, tenting it slightly in the middle so the cake doesn't touch the foil when it rises during baking. Bake 55 minutes to 1 hour (center should be set). Remove cake from oven, lift off foil, and run a sharp knife around the inside edge of the pan to loosen cake. Let the cake cool 1 hour, then refrigerate for 3 hours. While the cake is chilling, prepare the Chocolate Glaze.

5. After cake has chilled, remove the ring from around the pan. Using a rubber spatula, spread the glaze smoothly over the top of the cake, filling the depression in the middle of the cake (the glaze should not reach the edges). Return cake to the refrigerator for 1 more hour before serving.

• APPROXIMATE NUTRITIONAL CONTENT •
Calories: 477, Protein: 12g, Net Carbs: 9g, Fat: 43g, Cholesterol: 140mg, Sodium: 360mg

chocolate chip cheesecake

•••

ESTIMATED PREPARATION TIME: 15 minutes (plus at least 5 hours cooling/chilling time)
COOK TIME: 50 minutes • **SERVINGS:** 8

•••

THE COMBINATION OF sugar-free chocolate and real semi-sweet chocolate works wonders for the flavor of this cheesecake, and the mini chips on the top make for an eye-pleasing presentation.

for the crust:

cooking spray
5 chocolate graham cracker rectangles, crushed (about ¾ cup crumbs)
2 tablespoons butter, melted

for the cheese filling:

1 8-ounce packaged Neufchâtel cheese, softened
1 8-ounce package cream cheese, softened
2 eggs
¾ cup whipping cream
½ cup Splenda Granular sweetener
½ teaspoon vanilla extract
1 3-ounce bar sugar-free milk chocolate, chopped
2 tablespoons mini semi-sweet chocolate chips

1. Preheat the oven to 350°F.
2. *To make the crust:* Spray the bottom and sides of an 8-inch springform pan with cooking spray. In a small bowl, combine the graham cracker crumbs with the melted butter. Pat the mixture into the bottom of the pan, forming an even but thin crust. Bake crust 8 minutes; remove from oven to cool, but leave oven on. While crust is cooling, prepare cheese filling.
3. *To make the filling:* In a large mixing bowl, using an electric mixer on medium speed, blend together the softened cheeses and the eggs, scraping bowl occasionally, until smooth. Add the whipping cream, Splenda, and vanilla and mix until almost fluffy, about 5 minutes. Using a wooden spoon, stir in the chopped chocolate.
4. Pour filling into cooled crust; sprinkle the top with mini chocolate chips. Cover the top of the pan with foil, tenting it slightly in the middle so the cake doesn't touch the foil when it rises during baking and bake for 50 minutes.

5. Remove cake from oven, lift off foil, and run a sharp knife around the inside edge of the pan to loosen cake. Let the cake cool 1 hour, then remove the ring from around the pan. Refrigerate for 4 hours before serving.

• **APPROXIMATE NUTRITIONAL CONTENT** •
Calories: 325, Protein: 8g, Net Carbs: 7g, Fat: 27g, Cholesterol: 114mg, Sodium: 275mg

no-bake cookies and cream cheesecake

ESTIMATED PREPARATION TIME: 15 minutes (plus at least 6 hours chilling time)
COOK TIME: none • **SERVINGS:** 10

EASY AND SPECIAL enough for company. Try this cheesecake drizzled with a little Low-Carb Chocolate Sauce (page 197) for a more decadent dessert!

for the crust:

cooking spray
1 recipe Chocolate Graham Crust (page 62)

for the cheese filling:

½ cup boiling water
1 envelope plain gelatin
2 8-ounce packages cream cheese, softened
1½ teaspoons vanilla extract
½ cup whipping cream
½ cup Splenda Granular sweetener
6 sugar-free chocolate cream sandwich cookies, coarsely crumbled

1. *To make the crust:* Spray the bottom and sides of a 9-inch springform pan with cooking spray. Press the Chocolate Graham Crust mixture onto the bottom of the pan. Set crust aside while preparing filling.

2. *To make the cheese filling:* Pour the water into a small bowl, sprinkle the gelatin over the water, and let it sit while preparing the rest of the filling ingredients. In a large mixing bowl, using an electric mixer on medium speed, blend together the softened cheese and the vanilla extract, scraping bowl occasionally, until smooth. Add the whipping cream and mix on medium speed until very thick, about 2 minutes. Stir the gelatin and water to combine, then add it to the filling mixture, along with the Splenda. Mix on high speed until filling nearly doubles in volume and becomes stiff. Using a rubber spatula or wooden spoon, stir in the crumbled cookies.

3. Transfer filling to the crust, using a rubber spatula to smooth the top. Cover lightly with plastic wrap (don't let the wrap touch the filling surface), and refrigerate at least 6 hours or overnight. To serve, run a sharp knife around the inside edge of the pan to loosen cake, then remove the ring from around the pan.

• APPROXIMATE NUTRITIONAL CONTENT •
Calories: 379, Protein: 11g, Net Carbs: 3g, Fat: 37g, Cholesterol: 99mg, Sodium: 165mg

bite-sized cheesecakes

ESTIMATED PREPARATION TIME: 20 minutes (plus at least 3 hours cooling/chilling time)
COOK TIME: 15 minutes • **SERVINGS:** 12 servings (2 cakes per serving)

*L*IGHT ON CARBS, EASY, delicious, and versatile—what more could you want in a dessert? Choose your favorite extract flavor and you're in business! For variety, divide the cheesecake batter in half and make two different flavors (perfect for a party). These freeze well, for up to two weeks, so don't worry if you have "too many."

2 8-ounce packages cream cheese, softened
2 eggs
¼ cup whipping cream
½ cup Splenda Granular sweetener
1 to 1½ teaspoons favorite extract (such as lemon, cherry, banana, peppermint, etc.)
food coloring in an appropriate color (optional) (such as yellow for lemon cakes, etc.)
24 mini foil cupcake liners
24 vanilla wafer-type cookies
1½ cups Homemade Whipped Cream, for garnish (page 190)

1. Preheat the oven to 350°F. In a large mixing bowl, using an electric mixer on medium speed, blend together the softened cheese and the eggs, scraping bowl occasionally, until smooth. Add the whipping cream, Splenda, extract, and food coloring, if desired, and mix until almost fluffy, about 5 minutes.

2. On each of two baking sheets, place 12 of the cupcake liners, evenly spaced and not touching each other. Place a vanilla wafer cookie in the bottom of each cupcake liner. Using a tablespoon, carefully spoon the cream cheese mixture into each liner, filling them just to the rim (smooth the tops). Do not mound the mixture or it will spill over during baking.

3. Bake the cheesecakes for 15 minutes. Remove from oven and let cakes cool for 1 hour, then cover lightly with plastic wrap and refrigerate at least 2 hours. Garnish chilled cheesecakes with a piped rosette (or small dollop) of the Homemade Whipped Cream.

• APPROXIMATE NUTRITIONAL CONTENT •
Calories: 248, Protein: 4g, Net Carbs: 8g, Fat: 22g, Cholesterol: 108mg, Sodium: 154mg

pies and tarts

peanut butter cup pie

ESTIMATED PREPARATION TIME: 15 minutes (plus at least 2 hours chilling time)
COOK TIME: 8 minutes for crust • **SERVINGS:** 10

IF YOU LIKE peanut butter cup candies, you'll absolutely love this super-rich, super-creamy pie.

1 8-ounce package cream cheese, softened
1 cup low-carb peanut butter
⅔ cup Splenda Granular sweetener
¼ cup light cream
1 teaspoon vanilla extract
1 cup Homemade Whipped Cream (page 190)
4 sugar-free peanut butter cup candies, chopped
1 ounce sugar-free milk chocolate, chopped

1 recipe Chocolate Graham Crust, baked in a 9-inch pie plate and cooled (page 62)

1. In a medium mixing bowl, using an electric mixer on medium speed, mix the cream cheese with the peanut butter and Splenda until blended. Add the light cream and vanilla and mix again to blend, scraping bowl with a rubber spatula occasionally.

2. Using a rubber spatula, gently stir the Homemade Whipped Cream into the peanut butter mixture until blended and fluffy. Add the chopped peanut butter cups and stir again to distribute the candies throughout the filling.

3. Spoon the mixture into the prepared crust, smoothing the top with the spatula. Sprinkle the chopped chocolate over the top for garnish. Refrigerate pie at least 2 hours before serving.

• APPROXIMATE NUTRITIONAL CONTENT •
Calories: 475, Protein: 11g, Net Carbs: 9g, Fat: 44g, Cholesterol: 74mg, Sodium: 270mg

blueberry cream pie

ESTIMATED PREPARATION TIME: 15 minutes (plus at least 3 hours cooling/chilling time)
COOK TIME: 10 minutes, plus 8 minutes for crust • **SERVINGS:** 8

THIS PIE FEATURES two layers: a vanilla-spiked cream cheese layer and a generous layer of cinnamon-spiced blueberries. It's especially delicious when made with Maine's wild blueberries, which can be found frozen in most supermarkets.

for the cream layer:

1 8-ounce package cream cheese, softened
1/4 cup whipping cream
1/4 cup Splenda Granular sweetener
1/2 teaspoon vanilla extract

for the blueberry layer:

2/3 cup Splenda Granular sweetener
1/3 cup cold water
1 1/2 teaspoons Expert Foods' ThickenThin Not/Starch
1/4 teaspoon cinnamon
1/8 teaspoon salt
3 cups fresh or frozen blueberries (thaw frozen berries)
1/2 teaspoon vanilla extract

1 recipe Cinnamon-Almond Crust, baked in a 9-inch pie plate, and cooled (page 63)

1. *To make the cream layer:* In a medium mixing bowl, using an electric mixer on medium speed, blend the cream cheese, whipping cream, Splenda, and vanilla until smooth and combined. Using a rubber spatula, spread the cream layer over the cooled crust, making the first layer. Refrigerate the pie while preparing the blueberry layer.

2. *To make the blueberry layer:* In a medium, heavy saucepan, stir together the Splenda, water, thickener, cinnamon, and salt. Cook on the stove over medium heat, stirring occasionally, until thickened, about 2 minutes. Stir in blueberries and heat for another 2 minutes, then remove from heat and stir in the vanilla extract. Let the blueberry mixture cool for 10 minutes, then spread it over the cream layer using a rubber spatula. Refrigerate pie for 3 hours before serving.

• APPROXIMATE NUTRITIONAL CONTENT •
Calories: 333, Protein: 10g, Net Carbs: 10g, Fat: 28g, Cholesterol: 61mg, Sodium: 258mg

lemon meringue pie

ESTIMATED PREPARATION TIME: 15 minutes (plus at least 4 hours cooling/chilling time)
COOK TIME: 20 minutes, plus 15 minutes for crust • **SERVINGS:** 10

A CLASSIC PIE with a lot fewer carbs than the traditional version. You'll notice that I've used the traditional cornstarch here, and not a low-carb thickener. This is because the filling should be clear, and the thickeners tend to cloud fillings like this. If you don't mind the cloudiness, feel free to use the thickener instead.

1/3 cup cornstarch
1/8 teaspoon salt
1 cup Splenda, divided
1 1/2 cups water
4 eggs, room temperature, yolks and whites separated
1 tablespoon butter
2/3 cup freshly squeezed lemon juice
1 tablespoon grated lemon peel
1/4 teaspoon cream of tartar
2 tablespoons sugar

1 recipe "Traditional" Pie Crust, baked in a 9-inch pie plate, and cooled (page 64)

1. *To make the filling:* In a medium saucepan, whisk together the cornstarch, salt, and ¾ cup of the Splenda. Add the water and whisk until the cornstarch is dissolved. Turn the heat on to medium and cook, whisking constantly, until the mixture thickens and comes to a boil, about 5 minutes. Boil and stir 1 minute more, then turn off heat.
2. Place the egg yolks into a small bowl or a mug; beat them lightly with a fork. Take a small spoonful of the hot mixture and stir it into the egg yolks, then slowly pour the egg mixture back into the lemon mixture, whisking constantly and rapidly.
3. Turn the heat back on to medium and cook, whisking constantly, another 5 minutes until filling mixture is very thick. Turn off the heat, whisk in the butter, lemon juice, and lemon peel until well combined. Pour filling into the prepared crust; let pie cool on the counter while preparing the meringue.
4. Preheat the oven to 400°F.

5. *To make the meringue:* In a medium mixing bowl, using an electric mixer, beat the egg whites at high speed until foamy, about 1 minute. Add the cream of tartar and continue to beat until soft peaks form. Gradually add the remaining ¼ cup Splenda and the 2 tablespoons sugar to the egg whites; continue to beat until stiff peaks form.

6. Using a rubber spatula, spread the meringue over the top of the pie, being sure to spread it all the way to the edges (meringue must touch the crust or it will shrink when heated). Using the back of a spoon, swirl the meringue decoratively.

7. Bake 10 minutes, or until meringue is golden in color. Remove pie from oven and cool 1 hour. Refrigerate, uncovered, for 3 hours before serving.

• **APPROXIMATE NUTRITIONAL CONTENT** •
Calories: 169, Protein: 7g, Net Carbs: 14.5g, Fat: 9g, Cholesterol: 110mg, Sodium: 67mg

lime chiffon pie

CREAMY AND FLUFFY at the same time, the filling in this pie is slightly tart and oh-so-delicious. You could also make a lemon version; just use lemon juice and lemon peel instead of the lime juice and peel. Be sure to chill this sufficiently or the texture of the filling will suffer.

¼ cup cold water
1 packet unflavored gelatin
1 cup Splenda Granular sweetener, divided
⅛ teaspoon salt
1 teaspoon grated lime peel
½ cup freshly squeezed lime juice
4 eggs, yolks and whites separated
1 teaspoon sugar

1 recipe "Traditional" Pie Crust, baked in a 9-inch pie plate, and cooled (page 64)

1. Add the cold water to a small saucepan; sprinkle the gelatin over the water and let sit for 5 minutes, until gelatin softens. Whisk in ½ cup of the Splenda, the salt, lime peel, and lime juice until well blended. Add the egg yolks and whisk again to combine.

2. Place saucepan over medium heat and whisk slowly, until gelatin is dissolved (do not let filling boil), about 5 minutes. Turn off the heat and place the saucepan in the refrigerator for ½ hour, or until the mixture thickens slightly (it should drop in mounds from a spoon).

3. While waiting for the mixture to chill, beat the egg whites in a medium mixing bowl with an electric mixer on medium until foamy, about 3 minutes. Add the remaining ½ cup Splenda and the sugar. Turn the speed up to medium-high and beat until egg whites are fluffy, but not stiff, about 2 minutes more.

4. When the lime mixture is chilled, gently whisk the beaten egg whites into the juice mixture to combine. Spoon the mixture into the prepared pie crust and smooth the top with a rubber spatula. Refrigerate at least 3 hours before serving.

• **APPROXIMATE NUTRITIONAL CONTENT** •
Calories: 176, Protein: 10g, Net Carbs: 12g, Fat: 10g, Cholesterol: 133mg, Sodium: 71mg

chocolate cream pie

ESTIMATED PREPARATION TIME: 10 minutes (plus at least 2$\frac{1}{2}$ hours chilling time)
COOK TIME: 8 minutes for crust • **SERVINGS:** 8

THIS CHOCOLATE LOVER'S favorite features a crunchy chocolate crust filled with a rich, fluffy chocolate pudding and a topping of whipped cream. My family was more than happy to taste-test this recipe again and again!

for the chocolate layer:

1 1.4-ounce package sugar-free, fat-free instant chocolate fudge pudding mix
1 cup low-carb chocolate milk
$\frac{3}{4}$ cup whipping cream

for the whipped cream layer:

1 cup whipping cream
1 tablespoon Splenda Granular sweetener
$\frac{1}{2}$ teaspoon vanilla extract

Pinch cocoa powder for garnish

1 recipe Chocolate Graham Pie Crust (page 62), baked in a 9-inch pie plate, and cooled

1. *To make the chocolate layer:* In a small mixing bowl, whisk together the pudding mix and low-carb milk; set aside. In a medium mixing bowl, using an electric mixer, whip the cream until soft peaks form. Add reserved pudding mixture to the bowl with the cream and whisk until well combined. Refrigerate the pudding for 30 minutes. While the pudding is chilling, prepare the whipped cream layer.

2. *To make the whipped cream layer:* In a medium mixing bowl, using an electric mixer on medium-high speed, whip the cream, Splenda, and vanilla until stiff peaks form.

3. Assemble the pie by spreading the chilled pudding mixture over the crust using a rubber spatula, then spooning the whipped cream mixture over the pudding (the cream should not reach the edges of the pie) to create a nicely rounded mound of cream in the center. Sprinkle the top with a pinch of cocoa powder for garnish. Return the pie to the refrigerator for at least 2 hours before serving.

• APPROXIMATE NUTRITIONAL CONTENT •
Calories: 363, Protein: 5g, Net Carbs: 13g, Fat: 33g, Cholesterol: 90mg, Sodium: 297mg

coconut cream pie

THIS FLUFFY PIE contains coconut in several places—the crust, filling, and as a garnish—to ensure plenty of coconut flavor. Try the Banana Cream variation, too!

for the coconut layer:
1 1-ounce package sugar-free, fat-free instant vanilla pudding mix
1 cup low-carb whole milk (do not use 2% or skim)
1½ teaspoons coconut extract
¾ cup unsweetened coconut, toasted, divided
¾ cup whipping cream

for the whipped cream layer:
1 cup whipping cream
1 tablespoon Splenda Granular sweetener
½ teaspoon vanilla extract

1 recipe Coconut–Shortbread Cookie Crust, baked in a 9-inch pie plate, and cooled (page 66)

1. *To make the coconut layer:* In a small mixing bowl, whisk together the pudding mix, low-carb milk, coconut extract, and all but 1 tablespoon of the toasted coconut (reserve the remaining tablespoon for garnish). Set pudding mixture aside. In a medium mixing bowl, using an electric mixer on medium-high speed, whip the cream until soft peaks form. Add reserved pudding mixture to the bowl with the cream and whisk until well combined. Refrigerate for 30 minutes. While the pudding is chilling, prepare the whipped cream layer.

2. *To make the whipped cream layer:* In a medium mixing bowl, using an electric mixer on medium-high speed, whip the cream, Splenda, and vanilla until stiff peaks form.

3. Assemble the pie by spreading the chilled pudding mixture over the crust using a rubber spatula, then spooning the whipped cream mixture over the center of the pudding, spreading it almost to the edges, and creating a nicely rounded mound in the center. Sprinkle the reserved 1 tablespoon of toasted coconut over the top to garnish. Return the pie to the refrigerator for at least 2 hours before serving.

• **APPROXIMATE NUTRITIONAL CONTENT** •

Calories: 355, Protein: 4g, Net Carbs: 11g, Fat: 33g, Cholesterol: 95mg, Sodium: 333mg

variation

TO MAKE A BANANA CREAM PIE:

Use the Nutty Graham Crust (page 61) instead of the Coconut–Shortbread Cookie Crust. For the banana layer, substitute 1 package of sugar-free, fat-free instant banana cream pudding mix for the vanilla pudding mix; substitute banana extract for the coconut extract; omit the toasted coconut; and add 2 drops yellow food coloring, if desired. Preparation directions are otherwise the same as for the Coconut Cream Pie.

• **APPROXIMATE NUTRITIONAL CONTENT** •

Calories: 378, Protein: 10g, Net Carbs: 6g, Fat: 35g, Cholesterol: 96mg, Sodium: 206mg

layered butterscotch cream pie

ESTIMATED PREPARATION TIME: 15 minutes (plus at least 1 hour chilling time)
COOK TIME: 5 minutes, plus 15 minutes for crust • **SERVINGS:** 10

*Y*OU'LL ONLY NEED a small slice of this very rich pie. . . .

for the butterscotch layer:
1 1-ounce package sugar-free, fat-free instant butterscotch pudding mix
1¾ cups low-carb whole milk (not 2% or skim)

for the cream layer:
3 tablespoons cold water
1 packet unflavored gelatin
4 ounces cream cheese, softened
¼ cup Splenda Granular sweetener
1 teaspoon vanilla extract
1½ cups heavy cream
2 1-ounce sugar-free toffee bars, roughly chopped

1 recipe "Traditional" Pie Crust, baked in a 9-inch pie plate, and cooled (page 64)

1. *To make the butterscotch layer:* In a small mixing bowl, whisk together the pudding mix and low-carb milk until blended. Pour mixture into the prepared pie crust; chill in the refrigerator while you prepare the cream layer.

2. *To make the cream layer:* Pour the water into a small saucepan; sprinkle the gelatin over the water and let sit about 5 minutes, until softened. Turn the heat on to low and stir the mixture until the gelatin is completely dissolved. Turn off the heat and let the mixture cool while you proceed with the recipe.

3. In a medium mixing bowl, using an electric mixer on medium speed, blend the cream cheese with the Splenda and vanilla until smooth, about 2 minutes; set aside. In a large mixing bowl, using an electric mixer on medium-high speed, blend the cream until soft peaks form, about 4 minutes. Slowly pour in the gelatin mixture while continuing to mix, and beat until stiff peaks form.

4. Spoon the cream cheese mixture into the bowl with the whipped cream mixture; whisk gently until well blended. Add the chopped toffee and whisk again to combine. Spoon the cream mixture over the chilled butterscotch layer and spread it smooth with a rubber spatula. Return the pie to the refrigerator to chill for at least 1 hour before serving.

• APPROXIMATE NUTRITIONAL CONTENT •
Calories: 321, Protein: 9g, Net Carbs: 11g, Fat: 26g, Cholesterol: 90mg, Sodium: 213mg

cinnamon cheese tart
with a walnut crust

• •

ESTIMATED PREPARATION TIME: 20 minutes (plus at least 3 hours cooling/chilling time)
COOK TIME: 30 minutes, plus 8 minutes for crust • **SERVINGS:** 10

• •

*M*Y NEIGHBORS RAVED about this sophisticated tart. Its combination of a cinnamon cheesecake topping over a crunchy walnut crust is perfectly suited to a fall or winter meal.

1 8-ounce package cream cheese, softened

4 ounces Neufchâtel cheese, softened

2 eggs

$\frac{1}{2}$ cup whipping cream

$\frac{1}{3}$ cup Splenda Granular sweetener

$1\frac{1}{4}$ teaspoons cinnamon

$\frac{1}{2}$ teaspoon vanilla extract

1 recipe Nutty Graham Crust, made with walnuts, baked in a 9-inch tart pan with removable bottom, and cooled (page 61)

1. Preheat the oven to 350°F.
2. In a medium mixing bowl, using an electric mixer on medium speed, blend together the softened cheeses and the eggs until smooth, scraping the bowl occasionally. Add the remaining ingredients and mix until almost fluffy, about 5 minutes.
3. Pour filling into cooled crust. Cover the top of the pan with foil, tenting it slightly in the middle so the tart doesn't touch the foil when it rises during baking. Bake 25 to 30 minutes, or until set.
4. Remove the tart from the oven, lift off the foil, and let the tart cool for 1 hour on the counter. Refrigerate tart for at least 2 more hours; remove pan edge before serving.

• APPROXIMATE NUTRITIONAL CONTENT •
Calories: 302, Protein: 7g, Net Carbs: 9g, Fat: 27g, Cholesterol: 105mg, Sodium: 231mg

key lime tartlets

ESTIMATED PREPARATION TIME: 15 minutes (plus at least 1 hour chilling time)
COOK TIME: 5 minutes • **SERVINGS:** 5 (3 tartlets each)

FRESH KEY LIME juice is preferable in this recipe, as you truly get a better flavor from squeezing the tiny limes yourself. However, they can be hard to come by sometimes, in which case bottled key lime juice is fine. Regular lime juice won't deliver the same flavor at all, but in a pinch you can use it (you'll need to use fresh-squeezed; and increase the amount of juice to ⅓ cup and eliminate the water in the recipe). Traditionally, key lime pie is made with sweetened condensed milk, which mellows the tart juice considerably, but is also high in carbs. To keep the carbs low, I used the juice in a lime curd, which does pack a punch—but the whipped cream helps balance the tartness.

for the key lime curd:

⅔ cup Splenda Granular sweetener
¾–1 teaspoon Expert Foods' ThickenThin No/Starch
¼ cup freshly squeezed key lime juice
2 tablespoons water
2 tablespoons butter, diced
2 egg yolks, slightly beaten

1 2.1-ounce package frozen phyllo cups, thawed 10 minutes at room temperature
¾ cup Homemade Whipped Cream, for garnish (page 190)
Strips of lime peel, optional garnish

1. *To make the lime curd:* In a heavy, small saucepan, stir together the Splenda, thickener, lime juice, and water until blended. Add the butter and heat over a low flame. Whisk the mixture until butter melts. Turn the heat to medium and whisk constantly until mixture thickens, about 3 minutes. Quickly whisk in the beaten egg yolks and continue to whisk until mixture becomes thicker, about 1 minute. Remove from heat and let cool about 10 minutes.
2. Leave the phyllo cups in their plastic trays. Fill each phyllo cup using a small spoon. Place the tray of filled tartlets in the refrigerator for at least 1 hour, or until serving time.

3. Before serving, garnish each tartlet with a dollop of the whipped cream (if you like, you can place the cream in a plastic baggie, cut off a corner, and pipe the cream onto the tartlet for a nicer presentation); add a small strip of lime peel to the top of eat tartlet, if you wish.

• **APPROXIMATE NUTRITIONAL CONTENT** •

Calories: 261, Protein: 3g, Net Carbs: 10g, Fat: 24g, Cholesterol: 147mg, Sodium: 93mg

easy pear tart

ESTIMATED PREPARATION TIME: 10 minutes (plus 1 hour cooling time)
COOK TIME: 25 minutes, plus 8 minutes for crust • **SERVINGS:** 8

*L*OOKING FOR A nice way to take advantage of fall and winter pears? This is your answer! Be aware that the crust is very delicate, so take care when serving this tart—use a pie server.

2 medium, ripe pears (such as Anjou or Bartlett),
peeled, cored and sliced ¼-inch thick

for the topping:
½ teaspoon ground cinnamon
1 tablespoon finely chopped almonds
1 tablespoon Sugar Twin Brown Sugar
1 cup Homemade Whipped Cream (page 190) (optional garnish)

1 recipe Cinnamon–Almond Crust, baked in a 9-inch tart pan with removable bottom, and cooled
(page 63)

1. Preheat oven to 400°F. Arrange pear slices, overlapping each other slightly, in a circle pattern on the cooled crust. Fill in gaps with smaller pear slices, or cut slices to fit as needed. Entire crust should be covered with slices.
2. In a small bowl, stir together the topping ingredients; sprinkle topping over the pears evenly. Bake tart for 25 minutes, or until pears are fork-tender.
3. Remove tart from the oven and let cool 1 hour. Remove pan edge before serving with Homemade Whipped Cream, if desired.

• APPROXIMATE NUTRITIONAL CONTENT •
Calories: 199, Protein: 8g, Net Carbs: 6g, Fat: 16g, Cholesterol: 20mg, Sodium: 130mg

cook's tip
This tart is best served at room temperature, on the day it's made.

nutty graham crust

THIS CRUST (and its variations) is nice for firm-textured pies that don't need a lot of "support," such as ice cream pies or cheese pies.

●

5 large graham cracker rectangles, crushed (about ¾ cup crumbs)
¾ cup almond meal/flour (or very finely chopped almonds)
4 tablespoons butter, melted
cooking spray

●

1. Preheat oven to 350°F. In a small bowl, combine all ingredients together. Spray pie plate (9-inch) or tart pan (9-inch round or 11-by-7-inch rectangle) with cooking spray, then pat crust mixture into bottom and up the sides of pan.
2. Bake crust for 8 minutes, until nicely browned. Let crust cool before filling.

• APPROXIMATE NUTRITIONAL CONTENT •
Calories: 158, Protein: 3g, Net Carbs: 9.5g, Fat: 12g, Cholesterol: 16mg, Sodium: 127mg

---

variation

Ground or very finely chopped pecans or walnuts can be substituted for the almonds in this recipe—a food processor or clean coffee grinder makes quick work of the nuts.

chocolate graham crust

ESTIMATED PREPARATION TIME: 5 minutes
COOK TIME: 8 minutes • **SERVINGS:** 8

*W*HEN YOU WANT your pie crust to contribute a little chocolate flavor, this is the recipe to turn to.

5 large chocolate graham cracker rectangles, crushed (about ¾ cup crumbs)
¾ cup almond meal/flour (or very finely chopped almonds)
4 tablespoons butter, melted
cooking spray

1. Preheat oven to 350°F. In a small bowl, combine all ingredients together. Spray pie plate (9-inch) or tart pan (9-inch round or 11-by-7-inch rectangle) with cooking spray, then pat crust mixture into bottom and up the sides of pan.
2. Bake crust for 8 minutes. Let crust cool before filling.

• **APPROXIMATE NUTRITIONAL CONTENT** •
Calories: 153, Protein: 3g, Net Carbs: 7g, Fat: 13g, Cholesterol: 16mg, Sodium: 84mg

cinnamon—almond crust

ESTIMATED PREPARATION TIME: 5 minutes
COOK TIME: 8 minutes • **SERVINGS:** 10

THIS VERSATILE CRUST has just a touch of cinnamon to nicely complement fruit fillings, such as with the Three-Layer Blackberry Bars (page 78) or the Easy Pear Tart (page 60).

1 cup almond meal/flour (or very finely chopped almonds)
½ cup Atkins Bake Mix
2 tablespoons whole wheat flour
1 tablespoon Splenda Granular sweetener
1 teaspoon ground cinnamon
5 tablespoons butter, melted
cooking spray

1. Preheat oven to 350°F. In a small bowl, combine all ingredients. Spray pie plate (9-inch) or tart pan (9-inch round or 11-by-7-inch rectangle) with cooking spray, then pat crust mixture onto bottom and slightly up sides of pan.
2. Bake crust for 8 minutes, until nicely browned. Let crust cool before filling.

• **APPROXIMATE NUTRITIONAL CONTENT** •
Calories: 140, Protein: 6g, Net Carbs: 2g, Fat: 12g, Cholesterol: 16mg, Sodium: 104mg

variation

Feel free to substitute 1 cup of ground or very finely chopped walnuts or pecans for the almonds in this recipe.

"traditional" pie crust

ESTIMATED PREPARATION TIME: 10 minutes
COOK TIME: 12–18 minutes • SERVINGS: 8–10

IT'S NOT "JUST like Grandma used to make," but it's a pretty good imitation—and it's lower in carbs, too. This crust rolls out easily and bakes up nicely. Note that this recipe does not make a crust large enough for a "deep dish" pie.

1/2 cup wheat gluten (plus about 2 tablespoons extra to sprinkle on counter/rolling pin)
1/2 cup whole wheat pastry flour
1/4 cup almond meal/flour (or very finely chopped almonds)
1 tablespoon Splenda Granular sweetener
1 egg yolk, beaten
3 tablespoons cold shortening
3–4 tablespoons very cold water
cooking spray

1. Preheat oven to 375°F. In a small mixing bowl, stir together the gluten, pastry flour, almonds, and Splenda. Using a fork, stir in the egg yolk, then the shortening, using the fork to mash the shortening into the mixture until it forms coarse crumbs. Add the water, stirring it in 1 tablespoon at a time. Use only as much as needed to get the mixture to form a ball. Let the dough rest for a minute while you spray a pie plate (8-inch or 9-inch) with cooking spray.

2. Sprinkle 1 tablespoon wheat gluten over a clean counter, pastry board, or cutting board (to keep the pie crust from sticking). Sprinkle your rolling pin with a little wheat gluten as well, then roll the dough out with the rolling pin. Set the pie pan over the dough (upside down) in order to help you "measure" how large to roll out the dough. Keep rolling and measuring until the dough extends beyond the edge of the pie pan about 1½ inches. Remove the pie pan.

3. Using a spatula to help remove the pie crust from the counter, carefully fold the crust in half, then ease it into the prepared pan. Gently fit the crust into the pan (try not to stretch it).

4. Crimp the top edge of the crust as desired (use your fingers or a fork to finish the edge) and prick the crust on the bottom and sides with a fork. If the recipe calls for a "partially baked" crust, bake it for 12 minutes; for a "baked" crust, bake it for 15 minutes. If filling the crust before baking, follow the recipe directions for baking time.

• **EACH SERVING (8 SERVINGS PER PIE) CONTAINS APPROXIMATELY** •
Calories: 126, Protein: 6g, Net Carbs: 9g, Fat: 7g, Cholesterol: 27mg, Sodium: 1mg

• **EACH SERVING (10 SERVINGS PER PIE) CONTAINS APPROXIMATELY** •
Calories: 101, Protein: 5g, Net Carbs: 7g, Fat: 6g, Cholesterol: 21mg, Sodium: 1mg

coconut–shortbread cookie crust

ESTIMATED PREPARATION TIME: 5 minutes
COOK TIME: 8 minutes • **SERVINGS:** 10

CRUNCHY AND SWEET, this cookie crust is great with the Tangy Citrus-Coconut Tart (page 181), or any other fruit-based tart or pie you might create.

24 Murray's sugar-free ring-shaped shortbread cookies, crushed
½ cup unsweetened coconut
5 tablespoons butter, melted
cooking spray

1. Preheat oven to 350°F. In a small bowl, combine all ingredients together. Spray pie plate (9-inch) or tart pan (9-inch round or 11-by-7-inch rectangle) with cooking spray, then pat crust mixture into bottom of pan.
2. Bake crust for 8 minutes, until nicely browned. Let crust cool before filling.

• **APPROXIMATE NUTRITIONAL CONTENT** •
Calories: 117, Protein: 1g, Net Carbs: 5g, Fat: 10g, Cholesterol: 16mg, Sodium: 102mg

cookies and bars

favorite peanut butter cookies

ESTIMATED PREPARATION TIME: 10 minutes (plus 10 minutes cooling time)
COOK TIME: 8 minutes • **SERVINGS:** 12 (1 cookie per serving)

THIS OLD-FASHIONED favorite fits easily into a low-carb diet. Keep them in a resealable container or tightly wrapped on a plate so they stay moist.

½ cup low-carb peanut butter

⅓ cup Sugar Twin brown sugar substitute

¼ cup cocktail peanuts, chopped

2 tablespoons sugar, divided

1 tablespoon plus 2 teaspoons Expert Foods' ThickenThin Not/Sugar

1 tablespoon Atkins Bake Mix

½ teaspoon baking Soda

1. Preheat oven to 350°F. In a medium mixing bowl, using an electric mixer on medium speed, blend together all ingredients, using just 1 tablespoon plus 1 teaspoon sugar (reserving remaining 2 teaspoons sugar in a small bowl).

2. Using a tablespoon measure, scoop dough into clean hands and roll into balls. Dip each ball of dough into the reserved 2 teaspoons sugar, coating just the top of the ball. Place each dough ball, sugar-side up, on a cookie sheet, spacing them about 2 inches apart.

3. Using the tines of a fork, make a crosshatch pattern on each dough ball, flattening the cookies to about ¼ inch thick. Bake 7 to 8 minutes. Let cookies cool 3 minutes on the cookie sheet before transferring them to a wire rack to cool completely.

• APPROXIMATE NUTRITIONAL CONTENT •
Calories: 102, Protein: 4g, Net Carbs: 4g, Fat: 8g, Cholesterol: 18mg, Sodium: 131mg

mocha drop cookies

ESTIMATED PREPARATION TIME: 10 minutes (plus 10 minutes cooling time)
COOK TIME: 10 minutes • **SERVINGS:** 20 (1 cookie per serving)

I ADORE THE chocolate–coffee flavor combination known as mocha. These cookies are easy to make and very satisfying—a nice way to indulge without really being naughty.

4 tablespoons cold water
1 tablespoon instant coffee crystals
1 8½-ounces package Atkins Quick Quisine Fudge Brownie Mix
1 egg
¼ cup vegetable oil
¼ cup Atkins Bake Mix
cooking spray
2½ ounces sugar-free dark chocolate, broken into individual small squares

1. Preheat the oven to 350°F. In a small mixing bowl, stir together the water and coffee crystals until dissolved. Using a wooden spoon, stir in the brownie mix, egg, oil, and Atkins Bake Mix; stir thoroughly to combine (the mixture will be very thick and sticky). Let the mixture rest for a minute while you lightly coat two cookie sheets with cooking spray.

2. Using a tablespoon measure, scoop the dough onto the prepared cookie sheets, spacing the cookies about 2 inches apart. Bake cookies for 10 minutes. Remove from the oven and immediately place a small square of sugar-free chocolate on each cookie, pressing it down gently into the cookie.

3. Let the cookies cool 1 minute on the cookie sheet before transferring them to a wire rack to cool completely.

• APPROXIMATE NUTRITIONAL CONTENT •
Calories: 82, Protein: 2g, Net Carbs: 5.5g, Fat: 4g, Cholesterol: 11mg, Sodium: 58mg

chocolate chunk cookies

ESTIMATED PREPARATION TIME: 10 minutes (plus 10 minutes cooling time)
COOK TIME: 15 minutes • **SERVINGS:** 12 (1 cookie per serving)

IF YOU'VE BEEN missing homemade chocolate chip cookies, this recipe should calm your cravings. Full of big chocolate chunks, these cookies are good-sized (not teeny like many packaged low-carb cookies), yet the recipe makes just a dozen, to help you keep from overdoing it!

cooking spray
⅓ cup butter, softened
¼ cup Sugar Twin brown sugar substitute
3 tablespoons Splenda Granular sweetener
3 tablespoons sugar
1 egg
1½ teaspoons vanilla extract
¼ cup whole wheat flour
¼ cup wheat gluten
¼ cup all-purpose white flour
½ teaspoon baking powder
¼ teaspoon baking soda
⅛ teaspoon salt
1 3-ounce bar sugar-free bittersweet chocolate, roughly chopped

1. Preheat oven to 325°F. Spray a cookie sheet lightly with the cooking spray and set aside.
2. In a medium mixing bowl, using an electric mixer on medium speed, blend the butter, Sugar Twin, Splenda, and sugar together until smooth, about 1 minute. Add the egg and vanilla extract, and mix again until combined, scraping bowl with a rubber spatula occasionally.
3. In a small bowl, gently stir together the flours, baking powder, baking soda, and salt. Add the flour mixture to the butter mixture and mix on low speed until the dry ingredients are incorporated, then increase mixer speed to medium and blend another 2 minutes, until smooth. Using a wooden spoon, stir in chocolate chunks.

4. Using a tablespoon measure, scoop dough onto the prepared cookie sheet. Bake cookies for 13 to 15 minutes, or until lightly browned. Remove them from the oven and let cool 1 minute on the cookie sheet before transferring them to a wire rack to cool completely.

• APPROXIMATE NUTRITIONAL CONTENT •
Calories: 121, Protein: 3g, Net Carbs: 8g, Fat: 8g, Cholesterol: 30mg, Sodium: 123mg

easy ginger disks

ESTIMATED PREPARATION TIME: 10 minutes (plus 10 minutes cooling time)
COOK TIME: 11 minutes • **SERVINGS:** 18 (1 cookie per serving)

A GOOD, SOFT ginger cookie is hard to resist, and so far there are none on the supermarket shelves, so I created this quick and easy cookie.

cooking spray
2 tablespoons low-carb skim milk
1 tablespoon water
3 tablespoons butter, melted
1 8-ounce package Sweet'N Low no-sugar-added gingerbread cake mix
2 tablespoons sugar
1 teaspoon cinnamon

1. Preheat the oven to 350°F. Lightly coat two cookie sheets with cooking spray and set aside. In a medium mixing bowl, using an electric mixer on medium-low speed, mix the milk, water, butter, and cake mix until blended; set aside. In a small bowl, stir together the sugar and cinnamon.
2. Using a tablespoon measure, scoop the dough and roll into balls with clean hands. Roll the balls in the sugar-cinnamon mixture, then place the cookies on the prepared cookie sheets, spacing them about 2 inches apart.
3. Bake cookies for 11 minutes. Let the cookies cool 1 minute on the cookie sheet before transferring them to a wire rack to cool completely.

• **APPROXIMATE NUTRITIONAL CONTENT** •
Calories: 68, Protein: 1g, Net Carbs: 7g, Fat: 3g, Cholesterol: 5mg, Sodium: 30mg

maple nut cups

PECAN PIE IS generally made with lots of corn syrup—not exactly low-carb. These little nut cups are like miniature pecan pies in taste but are much lower in carbs. They make a nice addition to a party cookie platter. If you'd like, cashews can be used instead of the pecans for an interesting twist.

for the filling:

1 cup toasted pecans (or cashews), finely chopped

3 tablespoons Sugar Twin brown sugar substitute

2 tablespoons sugar-free maple syrup

1 egg yolk

2 teaspoons Expert Foods' ThickenThin Not/Sugar

$1/4$ teaspoon vanilla extract

$1/8$ teaspoon maple extract

1 2.1-ounce package frozen phyllo cups, thawed 10 minutes at room temperature

15 toasted pecan halves (or toasted whole cashews), garnish

1. Preheat the oven to 350°F.
2. *To make the filling:* In a medium mixing bowl, stir together all filling ingredients until well combined.
3. Place the phyllo cups on a rimmed cookie sheet. Using a teaspoon measure, scoop the nut mixture into each cup, filling to the top. Gently press a pecan half into the top of each filled cup to garnish.
4. Bake the cups for 15 minutes, then let cool at least 10 minutes before serving.

• APPROXIMATE NUTRITIONAL CONTENT •
Calories: 106, Protein: 2g, Net Carbs: 4g, Fat: 10g, Cholesterol: 14mg, Sodium: 17mg

coconut macaroons

ESTIMATED PREPARATION TIME: 5 minutes (plus ½ hour cooling time)
COOK TIME: 20 minutes • **SERVINGS:** 12 (1 cookie per serving)

𝒰NLIKE MANY A store-bought macaroon, these are moist inside—not at all dried out. For a more decadent treat, dip them in chocolate (see variation).

cooking spray
¾ cup Splenda Granular sweetener
½ cup unsweetened coconut milk
2 egg whites, at room temperature
1 cup unsweetened coconut
1 tablespoon Atkins Bake Mix
pinch of salt

1. Preheat the oven to 325°F. Coat a cookie sheet with cooking spray and set aside. In a medium mixing bowl, using a spoon, stir together the Splenda, coconut milk, and egg whites until blended.
2. In a small bowl, using a fork, stir together the coconut, Atkins Bake Mix, and salt, making sure that no lumps of the Bake Mix remain. Add the mixture to the wet ingredients and stir until combined.
3. Using a tablespoon measure, drop the dough onto the prepared baking sheet, spacing the cookies 1 inch apart (they don't spread). Bake for 20 minutes, then transfer the cookies to a wire rack to cool.

• APPROXIMATE NUTRITIONAL CONTENT •
Calories: 62, Protein: 2g, Net Carbs: 0g, Fat: 6g, Cholesterol: 0mg, Sodium: 34mg

CHOCOLATE-DIPPED COCONUT MACAROONS

Prepare the macaroons as above. When cookies are completely cooled, melt one 3-ounce bar sugar-free dark chocolate (chopped) and half of a 3-ounce bar sugar-free milk chocolate (chopped) in a microwavable bowl on LOW for 2 to 3 minutes. (The chocolate will not appear to be melted, so you'll have to stir it to check.) Stir the chocolate until smooth. Working with one cookie at a time, carefully dip the macaroon into the melted chocolate, coating just the top of the cookie with chocolate. Transfer dipped cookies to a piece of waxed paper and let them sit at room temperature until chocolate hardens, about 45 minutes.

• **APPROXIMATE NUTRITIONAL CONTENT** •
Calories: 107, Protein: 2g, Net Carbs: 0g, Fat: 9g, Cholesterol: 0mg, Sodium: 37mg

whoopie pies

●●●●●●●●●●●●●●●●●●●●●●●●●●●●●●●●●●●●●

ESTIMATED PREPARATION TIME: 15 minutes (plus $1/2$ hour cooling time)
COOK TIME: 10 minutes • **SERVINGS:** 8 (1 per serving)

●●●●●●●●●●●●●●●●●●●●●●●●●●●●●●●●●●●●●

HERE IN MAINE you can find these large filled cookies at every diner and bakery. Many places (including many in other states) claim to have invented the Whoopie Pie, but as far as I know, this is the first recipe for a low-carb Whoopie Pie! Unlike those that you'll find commercially made, these are very moist, giving the chocolate cookies more flavor than usual. For the best texture and flavor, eat these the day they're made.

●

for the cookies:
cooking spray
1 $8^1/2$-ounce package Atkins Quick Quisine Fudge Brownie Mix
1 egg
$1/4$ cup vegetable oil
2 tablespoons Atkins Bake Mix
$1/4$ cup oil

for the filling:
2 ounces cream cheese, softened
$1/2$ cup Sweet'N Low sugar-free white frosting mix
1 teaspoon vanilla extract
1 tablespoon plus $1/2$ cup whipping cream
12 La Nouba sugar-free marshmallows, quartered

●

1. Preheat the oven to 350°F.
2. *To make the cookies:* Lightly coat two cookie sheets with cooking spray and set aside. In a small mixing bowl, stir together all the cookie ingredients until well mixed. Using a tablespoon measure, drop the dough onto the prepared sheets, making 16 mounds of equal size (8 to a sheet). Try to make the dough mounds as round as possible.
3. Bake the cookies for 10 minutes, then remove from the oven and let them cool on the cookie sheets for 2 minutes before transferring them to a wire rack to cool completely. While cookies are cooling, prepare the filling.
4. *To make the filling:* In medium mixing bowl, using an electric mixer on medium speed, blend the cream cheese with the frosting mix, vanilla, and 1 tablespoon

whipping cream until mixed (it will be very thick). Add the remaining ½ cup cream and mix on low speed until smooth, scraping bowl with a rubber spatula occasionally. Using a wooden spoon, stir in the marshmallow pieces. Refrigerate filling until cookies are completely cool.

5. *To assemble the whoopie pies:* Pair up the cooled cookies, matching them in size and shape as best you can. Working with one cookie at a time, scoop a heaping tablespoon of filling onto the flat underside of a cookie, then top with its "matched" cookie. Place finished whoopie pies on a serving platter; continue with the remaining cookies and filling until you've made a total of 8 pies. Cover the whoopie pies lightly with plastic wrap and refrigerate until serving time. If you like, you can remove the whoopie pies from the refrigerator for about 15 minutes before serving, so they warm up a little (but do NOT microwave them!)

• APPROXIMATE NUTRITIONAL CONTENT •
Calories: 295, Protein: 5g, Net Carbs: 15g, Fat: 18g, Cholesterol: 57mg, Sodium: 169mg

three-layer blackberry bars

ESTIMATED PREPARATION TIME: 15 minutes (plus at least 1½ hours cooling/chilling time)
COOK TIME: 8 minutes for the crust • **SERVINGS:** 15 (1 bar per serving)

THESE SPECIAL BARS look fancy enough for a dinner party dessert, especially when served with a few fresh blackberries alongside.

for the blackberry layer:
¼ cup cold water
1–1½ tablespoons Expert Foods' ThickenThin Not/Sugar
1 12.75-ounce jar Smucker's sugar-free, "light" blackberry preserves

for the cheese layer:
1 8-ounce package cream cheese, softened
1 egg
2 tablespoons Splenda Granular sweetener
½ teaspoon vanilla extract
½ teaspoon lemon juice

2 tablespoons white chocolate chips, chopped, for garnish

1 recipe Cinnamon-Almond Crust, baked in a 11-by-7-inch tart pan with removable bottom, and cooled (page 63)

1. Preheat oven to 350°F.
2. *To make the blackberry layer:* In a small mixing bowl, using a fork, mix together the water, Not/Sugar, and jam until combined; set aside.
3. *To make the cheese layer:* In a medium mixing bowl, using an electric mixer on medium speed, mix the cream cheese with the egg until smooth and blended. Add the Splenda, vanilla, and lemon juice and mix for 1 minute to combine. Scrape bowl with a rubber spatula, then pour half the jam mixture into the cream cheese mixture; stir with a wooden spoon to blend. Set aside remaining half of jam mixture.
4. *To assemble the tart:* Pour the cream cheese mixture into the cooled crust, using a rubber spatula to spread it evenly to the edges. Refrigerate the bars for ½ hour, until firm. When firm, remove the bars from the refrigerator. Stir the remaining

jam mixture, then pour it over the chilled cheese layer, using a rubber spatula to spread it to the edges.

5. Garnish the bars with the chopped white chocolate, then return them to the refrigerator for 1 more hour before cutting and serving.

• **APPROXIMATE NUTRITIONAL CONTENT** •
Calories: 171, Protein: 6g, Net Carbs: 9g, Fat: 14g, Cholesterol: 42mg, Sodium: 52mg

amelia's angel cookies

ESTIMATED PREPARATION TIME: 15 minutes (plus 1/2 hour cooling time)
COOK TIME: 25 minutes • SERVINGS: 12 (1 cookie per serving)

MY DAUGHTER AMELIA and I created these delicious cookies and thought them so light that we decided they'd be suitable for angels to eat, hence the name. If you like meringue cookies, you'll Probably like these "enhanced" meringues, too.

2 egg whites, at room temperature
1 tablespoon sugar
1/8 teaspoon cream of tartar
1/4 cup Splenda Granular sweetener
1 tablespoon unsweetened cocoa powder
2 teaspoons Expert Foods' Cake-ability
1/4 teaspoon vanilla extract
1/4 cup unsweetened coconut
1/4 cup almond meal/flour (or very finely chopped almonds)
1 3-ounce bar sugar-free bittersweet chocolate, chopped

1. Preheat the oven to 250°F. Line a baking sheet with parchment paper and set aside.
2. In a medium mixing bowl, using an electric mixer on medium-high speed, blend the egg whites until foamy; add the sugar and cream of tartar and continue to mix until whites are stiff, but not dry, about 3 minutes more.
3. Add the Splenda, cocoa powder, Cake-ability, and vanilla extract and mix again, on medium speed, until blended, about 2 more minutes. Using a wooden spoon, stir in the coconut, almond meal, and chopped chocolate.
4. Using a tablespoon measure, drop generous spoonfuls of the mixture onto the parchment paper, spacing cookies about 1 inch apart (they don't spread much). Bake for 25 minutes, or until set and very lightly browned. Let cookies cool completely on the parchment, then carefully peel them off.

• APPROXIMATE NUTRITIONAL CONTENT •
Calories: 61, Protein: 2g, Net Carbs: 2g, Fat: 5g, Cholesterol: 0mg, Sodium: 19mg

pumpkin bars

. . . .

ESTIMATED PREPARATION TIME: 10 minutes (plus $1/2$ hour cooling time)
COOK TIME: 20 minutes • **SERVINGS:** 9 (1 bar per serving)

. . . .

A NICE FALL dessert, without the fuss of a pie. Even the kids will love these (though you may not want to share)!

cooking spray
$1/4$ cup Atkins Bake Mix
$1/4$ cup flour
2 eggs
$1/2$ cup pumpkin (not pumpkin pie mix)
$1/2$ cup Splenda Granular sweetener
$1/2$ teaspoon cinnamon
$1/4$ teaspoon ground cloves
pinch of nutmeg
$1/4$ teaspoon baking powder
$1/4$ teaspoon baking Soda
1 recipe Cream Cheese Frosting (page 196)

1. Preheat oven to 350°F. Spray an 8-inch square baking pan with cooking spray; set aside. In a medium mixing bowl, stir together the Atkins Bake Mix and flour. Add the eggs and pumpkin and whisk to blend; set aside.

2. In a small bowl, stir together the Splenda, cinnamon, cloves, nutmeg, baking powder, and baking Soda. Add the spice mixture to the reserved pumpkin mixture and stir to blend well.

3. Using a rubber spatula, spread batter into the prepared baking pan. Bake for 20 minutes, or until set but not dry. Let bars cool completely before frosting with Cream Cheese Frosting. Refrigerate any leftover bars.

• APPROXIMATE NUTRITIONAL CONTENT •
Calories: 128, Protein: 5g, Net Carbs: 5g, Fat: 10g, Cholesterol: 48mg, Sodium: 152mg

cranberry-orange cheesecake bars

. . . .

ESTIMATED PREPARATION TIME: 20 minutes (plus at least 2 hours cooling/chilling time)
COOK TIME: 30 minutes • **SERVINGS:** 24 (1 bar per serving)

. . . .

THIS TANGY BAR cookie is perfect for a winter occasion when you have a crowd, such as a New Year's open house or Super Bowl party. The flavors are seasonal, the recipe makes a lot of bars, and they're easily made up to one day ahead of time.

for the cake layer:

cooking spray

1 8-ounce package Atkins Quick Quisine Orange Cranberry Muffin & Bread Mix

2 eggs

½ cup oil

1 cup water

1 tablespoon orange juice concentrate (frozen)

for the cheese layer:

2 8-ounce packages cream cheese, softened

¼ cup whipping cream

2 eggs

⅓ cup Splenda Granular sweetener

1 tablespoon orange juice concentrate (frozen)

¾ cup fresh cranberries, chopped

2 teaspoons grated orange peel

1. Preheat oven to 350°F.
2. *To make the cake layer:* Spray a 10½-by-15½-inch jelly roll pan with cooking spray; set aside. In a medium mixing bowl, using a wooden spoon, stir together the muffin mix, eggs, and oil. Dissolve the orange juice concentrate in the water, then add it to the batter and mix to combine all ingredients. Using a rubber spatula, spread the batter evenly in the jelly roll pan, all the way to the edges.
3. Bake for 15 minutes in the top third of the oven, until very lightly browned. Let cool 15 minutes, but leave the oven on. While waiting for the cake layer to cool, prepare the cheese layer.
4. *To make the cheese layer:* In a medium mixing bowl, using an electric mixer on medium speed, blend together the cream cheese, whipping cream, and eggs until

very smooth and creamy, about 5 minutes, scraping bowl with a rubber spatula occasionally. Add the Splenda and orange juice concentrate; mix until blended. Using a wooden spoon, stir in the cranberries and orange peel; set aside.

5. Using a rubber spatula, gently spread the cheese mixture over the cooled cake layer. Bake 15 minutes in the upper third of the oven, until the cheesecake mixture is set. Let bars cool for ½ hour, then refrigerate for at least 1 hour before serving.

• APPROXIMATE NUTRITIONAL CONTENT •
Calories: 161, Protein: 7g, Net Carbs: 3g, Fat: 13g, Cholesterol: 60mg, Sodium: 142mg

lemon-strawberry cheesecake bars

ESTIMATED PREPARATION TIME: 20 minutes (plus at least 3 hours cooling/chilling time)
COOK TIME: 35 minutes • **SERVINGS:** 24 (1 bar per serving)

BERRIES AND LEMON go together well, so feel free to use your favorite type of berry (raspberries and blueberries taste equally delicious here). In summer, use fresh berries if you can, though either fresh or frozen (thawed) berries work well.

for the crust:
cooking spray
1 9-ounce package MiniCarb Lemon Burst Cookie Mix
2 eggs
1/4 cup plus 2 tablespoons softened butter
1/3 cup whipping cream
1/3 cup water

for the cheese layer:
1 8-ounce package Neufchâtel cheese, softened
1 8-ounce package cream cheese, softened
1/2 cup whipping cream
2 eggs
1/2 cup Splenda Granular sweetener
1 teaspoon vanilla extract
1 teaspoon lemon juice
1 1/2 cups chopped strawberries

1. Preheat oven to 350°F. Spray a 13-by-9-inch baking pan with cooking spray; set aside.
2. *To make the crust:* In a medium mixing bowl, using a wooden spoon, prepare the cookie mix according to package directions, using the eggs, butter, whipping cream, and water. Using a rubber spatula, spread the dough in the bottom of the prepared baking pan. Bake for 15 minutes in the top third of the oven, until set. Remove from the oven and let cool while preparing the cheese layer (leave oven on).
3. *To make the cheese layer:* In a medium mixing bowl, using an electric mixer on medium speed, mix together the cheeses, whipping cream, and eggs until very smooth and creamy, about 5 minutes, scraping bowl with a rubber spatula

occasionally. Add the Splenda, vanilla, and lemon juice and mix until blended. Using a wooden spoon, stir in the strawberries.

4. Using a rubber spatula, spread the cream cheese mixture over the cooled crust. Bake bars for 20 minutes in the upper third of the oven, until set. Let bars cool for ½ hour, then refrigerate for at least 2 hours before serving.

• APPROXIMATE NUTRITIONAL CONTENT •

Calories: 167, Protein: 5g, Net Carbs: 2.5g, Fat: 13g, Cholesterol: 57mg, Sodium: 137mg

chocolate-glazed raspberry brownies

ESTIMATED PREPARATION TIME: 8 minutes (plus at least 1 hour to cool)
COOK TIME: 40 minutes • **SERVINGS:** 12 (1 brownie per serving)

RASPBERRY AND CHOCOLATE is a classic flavor combination, and one that I happen to love. These easy brownies start with a mix and are topped with a thin layer of raspberry preserves and a coating of dark chocolate.

cooking spray
1 8½-ounce package Atkins Quick Quisine Fudge Brownie Mix
1 egg
⅓ cup vegetable oil
¼ cup water
⅓ cup Smucker's sugar-free, "light" raspberry preserves, whisked until free of lumps
1 3-ounce bar sugar-free dark chocolate, chopped

1. Preheat the oven to 350°F. Lightly coat the bottom only of an 8-inch square baking pan with cooking spray; set aside. In a small mixing bowl, using a wooden spoon, stir together the brownie mix, egg, oil, and water until well combined. Bake for 20 minutes.

2. Remove brownies from the oven (but leave oven on). Using a small rubber spatula, carefully spread the preserves over the brownies, being careful not to disturb the brownie batter. Return to the oven to bake for another 20 minutes.

3. Remove brownies from the oven and immediately sprinkle the chopped chocolate over the top of the brownies. Let sit 2 minutes, or until completely melted (the chocolate will not appear to be melted; you'll need to test it with a spatula to see if it's melted enough to spread). Spread the chocolate with a rubber spatula, completely covering the top of the brownies. Let glazed brownies sit at room temperature at least 1 hour before cutting and serving.

cook's tip

Leftover brownies may be refrigerated or left at room temperature. Refrigerating them will harden the chocolate topping, but it can be softened again by leaving the brownies at room temperature, or microwaving them briefly on LOW power.

• **APPROXIMATE NUTRITIONAL CONTENT** •

Calories: 143, Protein: 2g, Net Carbs: 10.5g, Fat: 8g, Cholesterol: 18mg, Sodium: 79mg

jam palmiers

ESTIMATED PREPARATION TIME: 10 minutes (plus 5 minutes cooling time)
COOK TIME: 15 minutes • **SERVINGS:** 15 (1 pastry per serving)

LIKE THE PASTRIES you'd get at a bakery, these palmiers are flaky, tender, and swirled with your choice of jam (apricot or blackberry are especially nice). I'll confess right here that I have eaten some for breakfast; they'd be nice with tea, too. Keep leftovers loosely covered with plastic wrap.

1 sheet (half of 17.3-ounce package) frozen puff pastry, thawed according to package directions

2 tablespoons Smucker's sugar-free, "light" preserves (choose your favorite flavor)

⅓ cup blanched, slivered almonds, finely chopped

2 teaspoons sugar

1. Preheat oven to 425°F. On a clean cutting board or work surface, unfold the puff pastry sheet. Using a small rubber spatula or butter knife, spread the jam evenly over the pastry, covering it completely. Sprinkle the chopped almonds evenly over the pastry.

2. Roll the long sides of the pastry toward each other until they meet in the center. With a serrated knife, cut the pastry crosswise into 15 ½-inch-thick slices (the slices will look a little like a butterfly shape). Lay the slices on ungreased cookie sheets, spacing them 2 inches apart. Sprinkle the sugar over the tops of the cookies.

3. Bake for 12 to 15 minutes, until golden brown. Remove from the oven and immediately transfer them to a wire rack to cool, using a metal spatula. Let cool for 5 minutes before serving (they're good warm, or at room temperature).

• APPROXIMATE NUTRITIONAL CONTENT •
Calories: 84, Protein: 2g, Net Carbs: 7g, Fat: 5.5g, Cholesterol: 0mg, Sodium: 80mg

rum-raisin nut balls

ESTIMATED PREPARATION TIME: 5 minutes (plus 2 hours cooling time)
COOK TIME: 3 minutes • **SERVINGS:** 10 (1 ball per serving)

*W*ATCH OUT! IF your house is anything like mine, these little treats will get gobbled up in a hurry by everyone—whether they're minding their carbs or not! It's easy to see why: these rum-flavored chocolates are loaded with raisin bits and coated with nuts, and are quickly made using a microwave.

2 tablespoons whipping cream
2 teaspoons unsalted butter
1 3-ounce bar sugar-free milk chocolate, chopped
1½ ounces sugar-free dark chocolate, chopped
¼ teaspoon rum extract
2 tablespoons (unpacked) raisins, finely chopped
2 tablespoons almonds or pecans, finely chopped

1. In a small, microwavable bowl, combine the cream and butter. Microwave on MEDIUM power for 1 to 2 minutes, until mixture comes to a simmer.
2. Stir in chopped chocolates, rum extract, and raisin pieces until all ingredients are coated with chocolate. Let mixture sit until firm and cool enough to handle, about 15 minutes.
3. Using clean hands, form the mixture into 1-inch balls. Roll each ball in the chopped nuts, then place the balls on a serving plate and let them sit at room temperature for about 1½ hours, until firm. To keep the balls for up to 1 week, place them in a covered container and refrigerate. To serve, bring them to room temperature, as they harden significantly in the refrigerator.

• APPROXIMATE NUTRITIONAL CONTENT •
Calories: 88, Protein: 1g, Net Carbs: 1g, Fat: 7g, Cholesterol: 6mg, Sodium: 8mg

no-bake buckeyes

BUCKEYES—THOSE TASTY little peanut butter balls dipped in chocolate—usually appear on cookie trays at holiday time, but they're delicious any time of year. Like other Buckeye recipes, these require no baking; but unlike other recipes, this one is sugar-free!

for the cookies:
¾ cup Splenda
2 tablespoons cornstarch
½ cup dry milk powder
½ cup low-carb peanut butter
4 tablespoons (½ stick) butter, very soft (but not melted)

for the chocolate coating:
1 3-ounce bar sugar-free dark or bittersweet chocolate, chopped
1 teaspoon shortening

1. *To make the cookies:* In a blender, food processor, or mini food chopper, combine the Splenda and the cornstarch; process until mixture becomes a fine powder, about 30 seconds to 1 minute. Transfer mixture to a small mixing bowl and stir in the dry milk powder. Using a fork, mix the peanut butter and softened butter into the dry ingredients. Continue to mix until all ingredients are blended and moist. Using a tablespoon, scoop the dough into your clean hands, and shape into balls. Place the balls on a sheet of waxed paper and set aside.

2. *To make the chocolate coating:* In a small, microwavable bowl, combine the chopped chocolate with the shortening. Microwave on LOW power for 2 minutes, until chocolate is melted (stop to stir and check it halfway through). Stir chocolate and shortening together until blended.

3. Working with one cookie at a time, hold the ball with your fingers and dunk it into the melted chocolate, so that the chocolate reaches about three-fourths of the way up the cookie. Gently scrape to remove excess chocolate, and place the cookie back on the waxed paper. Repeat with the remaining cookies and chocolate. Let the cookies sit at room temperature until the chocolate is set, about 1 hour. Store cookies in the refrigerator, loosely covered.

• **APPROXIMATE NUTRITIONAL CONTENT** •
Calories: 144, Protein: 4g, Net Carbs: 4g, Fat: 12g, Cholesterol: 11mg, Sodium: 105mg

chocolate
creations

double-chocolate cheesecake bites

ESTIMATED PREPARATION TIME: 15 minutes (plus at least 4 hours cooling/freezing/chilling time)
COOK TIME: 45 minutes • **SERVINGS:** about 12 (2 pieces per serving)

$\mathcal{M}$ILK CHOCOLATE CHEESECAKE drenched in a dark chocolate coating—and only one gram of carbs per bite-sized treat! Great for when you just want a "little something," or to serve alongside fresh berries for guests.

for the cheesecake:
cooking spray
1 8-ounce package Neufchâtel cheese, softened
1 8-ounce package cream cheese, softened
3 eggs
$\frac{1}{4}$ cup whipping cream
$\frac{1}{4}$ cup Splenda Granular sweetener
1 3-ounce bar sugar-free milk chocolate, chopped

for the chocolate coating:
2 3-ounce bars sugar-free dark chocolate, chopped
2 teaspoons shortening

1. Preheat the oven to 350°F. Line a 9-by-9-inch baking pan with aluminum foil, extending it over the sides (this makes it easier to remove the cheesecake from the pan). Spray the foil with cooking spray; set aside.
2. *To make the cheesecake:* In a large mixing bowl, using an electric mixer on medium speed, blend together the softened cheeses and the eggs for about 3 minutes, until combined, scraping bowl occasionally. Add the whipping cream, and Splenda, and mix until very smooth and almost fluffy, about 5 minutes.
3. Place the chopped milk chocolate in a small, microwavable bowl. Microwave on LOW power for 1 to 2 minutes, or until melted (it may not appear to be melted, so stir with a spoon to check it). Add the melted chocolate to the cheesecake mixture and mix on LOW speed to combine well. Pour mixture into the foil-lined pan and bake for 45 minutes.
4. Remove from the oven and let the cheesecake cool for $\frac{1}{2}$ hour. Place cooled cheesecake in the freezer, covered with a piece of waxed paper, for 3 hours, until completely frozen.

5. When the cheesecake is frozen, remove it from the pan, using the overhanging foil to help lift it out. Flip the cheesecake over onto a clean cutting board and carefully pull off foil. Using a long, sharp knife, trim about ½ inch off each edge of the cheesecake square, to create a neat square (discard the edges, or snack on them!). Flip the cheesecake square back over and cut it into 4 long strips; then cut each strip into 6 pieces, creating 24 pieces total.

6. *To make the chocolate coating:* In a small, microwavable bowl, combine the chopped chocolate with the shortening. Microwave on LOW power for 3 minutes (stop halfway through to stir and check to see if it's melted). Stir the chocolate and shortening together to blend.

7. Working with one cheesecake bite at a time, hold the cheesecake bite with your fingers, and dunk it into the melted chocolate, so that the chocolate reaches up the sides of the cheesecake bite but doesn't completely cover it (the bottom will not be coated). Gently shake off any excess chocolate and place the cheesecake bite, chocolate-coated side up, on a baking sheet covered with waxed paper. Repeat with the remaining cheesecake bites and chocolate. Place the bites in the refrigerator for at least ½ hour, or until serving time.

• APPROXIMATE NUTRITIONAL CONTENT •
Calories: 248, Protein: 7g, Net Carbs: 1g, Fat: 22g, Cholesterol: 95mg, Sodium: 154mg

individual chocolate "lava" cakes

JUST LIKE YOU get in a restaurant, only these are very low in carbs! These soufflé-like cakes feature a soft, pudding-like center that oozes out when you dig in, erupting a little bit of chocolate sauce. They're especially wonderful when served with a dollop of Homemade Whipped Cream (page 190) or low-carb vanilla ice cream.

2 teaspoons plus 1/3 cup unsalted butter, softened

2 teaspoons sugar, divided

4 ounces sugar-free bittersweet chocolate, chopped

2 eggs, at room temperature

2 egg yolks, at room temperature

3 tablespoons Splenda Granular sweetener

1/4 teaspoon vanilla extract

1 teaspoon flour

1. Preheat the oven to 375°F if you'll be baking the cakes right away. Coat the insides of four 4-ounce, ovenproof custard dishes or ramekins with the 2 teaspoons soft butter. Sprinkle 1/2 teaspoon of sugar all over the inside of each dish; set aside.

2. In a small, heavy saucepan, over low heat, stir together the chocolate and 1/3 cup unsalted butter until combined. Remove from heat and set aside.

3. In a small mixing bowl, using an electric mixer on medium speed, mix the eggs and yolks with the Splenda and vanilla for about 6 minutes, until thickened slightly. Spoon about 1 tablespoon of the reserved chocolate mixture into the eggs; whisk until combined, then add the remaining chocolate and the flour to the egg mixture and whisk again until well blended. Divide the batter evenly between the four custard cups (they'll be about two-thirds full).

4. Place the custard cups on a baking sheet and bake for 11 to 13 minutes, or until the edges are puffed and dry cracks appear, but the centers of the cakes still jiggle when the baking pan is shaken gently. Remove cakes from the oven and serve immediately.

cook's tip

These cakes need to be served immediately after baking, so if this doesn't work out for you time-wise, feel free to prepare the recipe through Step 3 early in the day and then chill the cakes in the refrigerator (lightly covered) until about 1 hour before you're ready to bake them (this allows them to come to room temperature). Then bake as directed in the recipe.

chocolate espresso silk tart

ESTIMATED PREPARATION TIME: 10 minutes (plus at least 4 hours cooling/chilling time)
COOK TIME: 10 minutes • **SERVINGS:** 12

THE SMOOTH, RICH mocha filling and crunchy chocolate crust belie how easy this tart is to prepare. Serve slender wedges of this tart with a dollop of Homemade Whipped Cream (page 190) for a decadent ending to a special meal.

1 cup whipping cream
1 tablespoon Splenda Granular sweetener
2½ tablespoons instant coffee crystals (or 1 tablespoon instant espresso powder)
¼ teaspoon vanilla extract
1 3-ounce bar plus 2 ounces sugar-free bittersweet chocolate, chopped
1 3-ounce bar sugar-free dark chocolate, chopped

1 recipe Chocolate Graham Crust, baked in a 9-inch tart pan with removable bottom, and cooled (page 62)

1. In a medium microwavable bowl, stir together the cream, Splenda, and coffee crystals (or espresso powder). Microwave the mixture on MEDIUM power for 2 minutes, until it just reaches a simmer. Add the vanilla extract and chopped chocolate, stirring until chocolate is melted and mixture is smooth and shiny. Pour chocolate mixture into the cooled crust.
2. Refrigerate tart at least 4 hours; remove pan edge before serving.

• **APPROXIMATE NUTRITIONAL CONTENT** •
Calories: 259, Protein: 3g, Net Carbs: 6g, Fat: 24g, Cholesterol: 38mg, Sodium: 64mg

easy chocolate hazelnut mousse tartlets

ESTIMATED PREPARATION TIME: 15 minutes (plus at least 2 hours chilling time)
COOK TIME: none • **SERVINGS:** 15 (2 tartlets per serving)

IF YOU'RE SHORT on time but expecting a crowd, these tarts are your answer. They take just a few minutes to assemble but are fancy enough for company. If you'd like to add a small dollop of Homemade Whipped Cream (page 190) to each tartlet before garnishing, that would dress them up even more.

1 2.8-ounce package Nestlé milk chocolate mousse mix
⅔ cup light cream
3 tablespoons Atkins Sugar-Free Hazelnut Syrup
2 2.1-ounce packages frozen phyllo cups, thawed 10 minutes at room temperature (such as Athens)
30 whole hazelnuts, toasted (about 1½ ounces)

1. In a medium mixing bowl, using an electric mixer, prepare the mousse mix according to package directions, substituting light cream for the milk specified.
2. Stir in the hazelnut syrup with a rubber spatula, scraping down the sides of the bowl. Mix for 1 minute more on high speed to combine well.
3. Leave the phyllo cups in their plastic trays. Fill each phyllo cup using a small spoon, mounding the mousse slightly in the middle (you'll use about 1 tablespoon of mousse for each tartlet). Place the trays of filled tartlets in the refrigerator for at least 2 hours, or until serving time.
4. Just before serving, place 1 hazelnut in the middle of each tartlet, and transfer the tartlets to a serving tray.

• APPROXIMATE NUTRITIONAL CONTENT •
Calories: 108, Protein: 2g, Net Carbs: 9g, Fat: 6g, Cholesterol: 7mg, Sodium: 32mg

chocolate belgian waffles

ESTIMATED PREPARATION TIME: 5 minutes
COOK TIME: 5–10 minutes (depending on waffle iron instructions) • **SERVINGS:** 4

These waffles are quick and easy to make, and are a handy "base" for a variety of dessert creations. Try my suggestions, or create your own "signature" dessert.

½ cup Atkins Quick Cuisine Pancake & Waffle Mix
1 tablespoon plus 1 teaspoon unsweetened cocoa powder
1 egg
⅓ cup plus 2 tablespoons water
1 tablespoon vegetable oil
cooking spray

1. Preheat a Belgian waffle iron according to manufacturer's directions.
2. In a small mixing bowl, combine all ingredients except for the cooking spray, and whisk until smooth.
3. Spray waffle iron lightly with cooking spray. Drop waffle batter onto waffle iron by mounded tablespoons, using 2 tablespoons for each waffle. (The batter will not fill the waffle square; waffles will be round when cooked.) Cook waffles according to manufacturer's directions. Use cooked waffles immediately as a dessert "base" (see suggestions below), or cool them completely and refrigerate for use later in the day. Waffles may also be frozen, in a quart-sized freezer bag, for up to 2 weeks.

• **APPROXIMATE NUTRITIONAL CONTENT** •
Calories: 95, Protein: 8g, Net Carbs: 4g, Fat: 5g, Cholesterol: 53mg, Sodium: 149mg

Easy Waffle Desserts

WHIPPED CREAM WAFFLE

Top each Chocolate Belgian Waffle with ¼ cup Homemade Whipped Cream (page 190) and 1 teaspoon mini semi-sweet chocolate chips. Makes 4 desserts.

• **APPROXIMATE NUTRITIONAL CONTENT** •
Calories: 324, Protein: 9g, Net Carbs: 5g, Fat: 28g, Cholesterol: 135mg, Sodium: 171mg

DOUBLE-CHOCOLATE ICE-CREAM SANDWICH

Top a Chocolate Belgian Waffle with ½ cup softened Atkins Endulge Chocolate Ice Cream, then top with another waffle, pressing down slightly. Wrap the waffle sandwich with plastic wrap and refreeze until firm. Repeat with remaining 2 waffles, to make a total of 2 ice-cream sandwiches.

• **APPROXIMATE NUTRITIONAL CONTENT** •
Calories: 320, Protein: 18g, Net Carbs: 12g, Fat: 10g, Cholesterol: 112mg, Sodium: 333mg

chocolate truffles

ESTIMATED PREPARATION TIME: 3 minutes (plus 2 hours cooling time)
COOK TIME: 3 minutes • **SERVINGS:** 8 (2 truffles per serving)

SOMETIMES ALL YOU need to end a meal is a nice little piece of chocolate and a cup of coffee. These truffles fit the bill perfectly, as they're carb-free (and less than ½ a gram rounds down to zero in my world) and can be made ahead of time so they're ready when you are. They also make a nice gift for low-carbing friends. Try the flavor variations below, or create your own.

¼ cup whipping cream
1 tablespoon unsalted butter
2 3-ounce bars sugar-free dark chocolate, chopped
1 3-ounce bar sugar-free milk chocolate, chopped
2 tablespoons unsweetened cocoa powder

1. In a small saucepan, over medium-low heat, stir together the cream and butter until melted and blended, about 2 minutes. Turn off the heat and add the chopped chocolate, whisking until melted and smooth. Let the mixture cool until firm, but not hard (check periodically), about 2 hours.

2. Using clean hands, form the truffles by rolling a generous teaspoonful of chocolate mixture in your hands to make a 1-inch ball. Place finished balls on a piece of waxed paper.

3. Place the cocoa powder in a small bowl, then roll each truffle in the cocoa to coat the outside. Place truffles on a serving plate, or cover until serving time. To keep truffles for up to 1 week, place them in a covered container and refrigerate. To serve, bring the truffles to room temperature, as they harden significantly in the refrigerator.

• **APPROXIMATE NUTRITIONAL CONTENT** •
Calories: 178, Protein: 3g, Net Carbs: 0g, Fat: 15g, Cholesterol: 14mg, Sodium: 11mg

COCONUT TRUFFLES:

Whisk in ¼ teaspoon of coconut extract along with the chopped choco-late. Roll truffles in 2 tablespoons unsweetened shredded coconut.

• APPROXIMATE NUTRITIONAL CONTENT •
Calories: 183, Protein: 3g, Net Carbs: 0g, Fat: 15g, Cholesterol: 14mg, Sodium: 11mg

CINNAMON TRUFFLES:

Prepare the basic chocolate truffles, then roll them in a mixture of 1 table-spoon unsweetened cocoa powder and 1 tablespoon ground cinnamon.

• APPROXIMATE NUTRITIONAL CONTENT •
Calories: 179, Protein: 3g, Net Carbs: 0g, Fat: 15g, Cholesterol: 14mg, Sodium: 11mg

MINT TRUFFLES:

Whisk in ¼ teaspoon peppermint extract along with the chopped choco-late. Crush 5 sugar-free peppermint candies and roll truffles in the crushed candies.

• APPROXIMATE NUTRITIONAL CONTENT •
Calories: 184, Protein: 2g, Net Carbs: 0g, Fat: 14g, Cholesterol: 14mg, Sodium: 11mg

chocolate-covered marshmallows

ESTIMATED PREPARATION TIME: 5 minutes (plus 1 hour cooling time)
COOK TIME: 2 minutes • **SERVINGS:** 6 (2 marshmallows per serving)

CHOCOLATE-COVERED MARSHMALLOWS are one of my favorite candy-store treats, and they're no longer just a memory since I discovered sugar-free marshmallows! Although quite pricey, this recipe makes the most of the marshmallows. Each piece delivers that great combination of chewy, sweet marshmallow and dark chocolate.

1 3-ounce bar sugar-free dark chocolate, chopped
1 teaspoon shortening
12 La Nouba sugar-free marshmallows

1. In a small microwavable bowl, combine the chopped chocolate with the shortening. Microwave on MEDIUM power for 1½ to 2 minutes (stopping halfway through to stir and check to see if it's melted). Stir the melted chocolate and shortening together to blend.
2. Working quickly, with one marshmallow at a time, dip the marshmallow into the melted chocolate mixture, then flip it so that the entire marshmallow is coated (yes, your hands will get dirty!). Gently scrape off the excess chocolate on the rim of the bowl and transfer the coated marshmallow to waxed paper to dry. Repeat with remaining marshmallows and chocolate.
3. Let the coated marshmallows sit at room temperature for 1 hour to let the chocolate harden. Serve immediately, or store in a covered container at room temperature until serving time.

• APPROXIMATE NUTRITIONAL CONTENT •
Calories: 96, Protein: 2g, Net Carbs: 0g, Fat: 5g, Cholesterol: 0mg, Sodium: 1mg

chocolate-covered macadamias

ESTIMATED PREPARATION TIME: 2 minutes (plus 1 hour cooling time)
COOK TIME: 2 minutes • **SERVINGS:** 10 (about $\frac{1}{4}$ cup nuts per serving)

CHOCOLATE-COVERED MACADAMIAS are widely available in Hawaii but can be hard to find elsewhere. Although the nuts themselves are pretty expensive, you can comfort yourself by keeping in mind that making these treats at home is still a lot cheaper than tickets to Hawaii!

1 teaspoon shortening
3 tablespoons whipping cream
$4\frac{1}{2}$ ounces sugar-free dark chocolate, chopped
$2\frac{1}{2}$ cups roasted, salted whole macadamia nuts

1. In a small microwavable bowl, combine the shortening and cream. Microwave on MEDIUM power for 1 minute, stir to blend. Whisk in the chopped chocolate until melted and smooth.
2. Place the nuts in a medium mixing bowl and pour the melted chocolate over them. Using a slotted spoon, stir to coat the nuts with the chocolate. Lift the nuts out of the bowl with the slotted spoon and spread them on a large sheet of waxed paper, making one layer of nuts. Separate any nuts that are stuck together with two forks. Let the nuts sit for 1 hour to let the chocolate harden. Store in a covered container at room temperature for up to 1 week.

• APPROXIMATE NUTRITIONAL CONTENT •
Calories: 313, Protein: 3g, Net Carbs: 0.5g, Fat: 32g, Cholesterol: 6mg, Sodium: 89mg

puddings, custards, trifles

and more

butterscotch crème brûlée

ESTIMATED PREPARATION TIME: 10 minutes (plus at least 6 hours chilling time)
COOK TIME: 10 minutes • **SERVINGS:** 6

⌐HIS VERSION OF crème brûlée seems like a natural, given that the brown sugar topping of a crème brûlée has a butterscotch flavor to it anyway. Be sure to crush the candies very fine or they'll harden, rather than dissolve, when you add them to the cream.

2 cups light cream
¼ cup Splenda Granular sweetener
12 sugar-free butterscotch discs (such as Werther's), finely crushed
¼ teaspoon vanilla extract
7 egg yolks
12 teaspoons light brown sugar, divided

1. Preheat the oven to 325°F. In a medium saucepan, over medium heat, whisk together the cream and Splenda. When mixture is hot (after about 3 minutes of cooking time) add the crushed candies, whisking briskly to dissolve them. Bring mixture to a simmer, whisking constantly. Remove from heat and whisk in the vanilla; set aside.

2. In a medium mixing bowl, using a whisk, break up the egg yolks slightly (no need to whip them at all). Slowly whisk in the reserved cream mixture until blended. Position a fine sieve over a plastic pitcher; pour the mixture into the pitcher through the sieve to strain it.

3. Place six 4-ounce custard cups or ramekins into a baking pan. Add about 1 inch of hot water to the pan (take care not to get it into the cups). Carefully pour the crème brûlée mixture into the custard cups, dividing it evenly. Transfer the pan to the oven and bake for 45 minutes, or until the center of the custards jiggle just slightly when the pan is gently shaken. Remove the custards from the water bath and let them cool on the counter to room temperature. Cover with plastic wrap and refrigerate at least 6 hours (or up to 2 days).

4. When ready to serve, sprinkle 2 teaspoons of brown sugar over each portion, spreading it gently with your fingers to make a thin, even layer. Position the oven rack about 4 inches below the broiler; set oven to a medium broil heat. Place the custards on a baking sheet and broil about 1 minute, or until the sugar is melted,

golden brown, and bubbling. Keep your eye on them: they burn quickly. Remove from the broiler and let the custards sit at room temperature to allow the sugar to harden to a "crust" before serving.

• APPROXIMATE NUTRITIONAL CONTENT •
Calories: 263, Protein: 5g, Net Carbs: 9g, Fat: 22g, Cholesterol: 303mg, Sodium: 65mg

easy vanilla panna cotta

ESTIMATED PREPARATION TIME: 5 minutes (plus at least 2 hours chilling time/not more than 24 hours)
COOK TIME: 8 minutes • **SERVINGS:** 6

𝒱ANILLA *PANNA COTTA* is usually made from a vanilla bean, which does give it a great, true vanilla flavor. However, the beans can be expensive and the process is often more complicated than anyone has time for. So, as long as you're using real vanilla extract (not imitation vanilla), you'll get a nice result from this recipe (though there won't be flecks of vanilla bean in the finished product). If you want vanilla bean flecks, you could use half the amount of vanilla extract and a tiny bit of vanilla bean paste (available from gourmet stores and specialty baking catalogs) to get the flecks without the hassle of dealing with the beans. This vanilla version is especially nice with berries or Apricot Sauce (page 199).

2 cups whipping cream
1 packet unflavored, unsweetened gelatin
1/3 cup Splenda Granular sweetener
1 1/2 teaspoons vanilla extract

1. Pour the cream into a medium saucepan. Sprinkle the gelatin over the surface of the cream and let it sit for 5 minutes. Turn the heat to medium-low and whisk the gelatin and cream together. Add the Splenda and whisk until blended and no gelatin lumps remain. Continue to cook, whisking slowly and frequently, until steam rises from the cream but it's not simmering. Remove from heat and whisk in the vanilla extract.

2. Carefully pour the mixture into six 4-ounce custard cups. Refrigerate the custards for 2 hours.

3. Before serving, remove *panna cotta* from the refrigerator and let it sit at room temperature for 10 minutes, to ease removal from the custard cups. To serve, carefully run a sharp paring knife around the inside edge of each custard cup to loosen the *panna cotta*. Invert each cup onto a dessert plate and shake until the custard is released.

• APPROXIMATE NUTRITIONAL CONTENT •
Calories: 280, Protein: 3g, Net Carbs: 2g, Fat: 29g, Cholesterol: 109mg, Sodium: 32mg

Panna cotta may be refrigerated longer than 2 hours, but should be served within 24 hours of making it. If you're not serving right away, place plastic wrap directly on the surface of the *panna cotta* after it has chilled for 2 hours.

kahlúa panna cotta

ESTIMATED PREPARATION TIME: 5 minutes (plus at least 2 hours chilling time/not more than 24 hours)
COOK TIME: 8 minutes • **SERVINGS:** 6

PANNA COTTA, THE current darling of the restaurant dessert menu, means "cooked cream." It doesn't sound like much, and in fact, it is quite a simple concoction—just cream, gelatin, sweetener, and a flavoring. However, the results are sublime. It's a custard like no other, supremely smooth, delicately flavored, and not overly sweet. It's a decidedly "adult" dessert, and a refreshing break from crème brûlée.

2 cups whipping cream
1 packet unflavored, unsweetened gelatin
1/3 cup Splenda Granular sweetener
1 tablespoon plus 2 teaspoons Kahlúa
1/4 teaspoon vanilla extract

1. Pour the cream into a medium saucepan. Sprinkle the gelatin over the surface of the cream and let it sit for 5 minutes. Turn the heat to medium-low and whisk the gelatin and cream together. Add the Splenda and whisk until blended and no gelatin lumps remain. Continue to cook, whisking slowly and frequently, until steam rises from the cream, but it's not simmering. Remove from heat and whisk in the Kahlúa and vanilla extract.

2. Carefully pour the mixture into six 4-ounce custard cups. Refrigerate the custards for 2 hours.

3. Before serving, remove *panna cotta* from the refrigerator and let it sit at room temperature for 10 minutes, to ease removal from the custard cups. To serve, carefully run a sharp paring knife around the inside edge of each custard cup to loosen the *panna cotta.* Invert each cup onto a dessert plate and shake until the custard is released.

• APPROXIMATE NUTRITIONAL CONTENT •
Calories: 291, Protein: 3g, Net Carbs: 4g, Fat: 29g, Cholesterol: 109mg, Sodium: 32mg

* * * * * * * * * * * * *

Panna cotta may be refrigerated longer than 2 hours but should be served within 24 hours of making it. If you're not serving right away, place plastic wrap directly on the surface of the *panna cotta* after it has chilled for 2 hours.

quick pumpkin pudding

ESTIMATED PREPARATION TIME: 10 minutes
COOK TIME: none • **SERVINGS:** 6 (about 1/2 cup per serving)

THIS IS AN easy dessert that's perfect for a casual fall gathering. It tastes like pumpkin pie, without the crust or the work. Be sure to serve it the day you prepare it, for best flavor and texture.

3/4 cup whipping cream
1 1/4 cups low-carb 2% milk
2/3 cup canned pumpkin (not pie filling mix)
1 1-ounce package sugar-free, fat-free instant vanilla pudding mix
1/2 teaspoon pumpkin pie spice

1. In a medium mixing bowl, using an electric mixer on medium-high speed, whip the cream until it forms soft peaks; set aside.
2. In another medium mixing bowl, using a whisk, combine the remaining ingredients until blended. Using a wooden spoon, gently stir in the reserved whipped cream, until just combined with the pumpkin mixture.
3. Spoon the pudding into individual dessert bowls and serve immediately, or cover and refrigerate up to 6 hours.

• APPROXIMATE NUTRITIONAL CONTENT •
Calories: 131, Protein: 7g, Net Carbs: 6g, Fat: 6g, Cholesterol: 13mg, Sodium: 183mg

easy mocha mousse

THIS "CHEATER'S" MOUSSE makes a lovely dessert for guests. It's easy to prepare, takes just a few ingredients, and keeps well in the refrigerator (ungarnished) for up to two days. Don't skip the garnish: it makes it pretty, and the crunchy cookies are a nice textural contrast to the mousse.

1 cup low-carb 2% milk
2 tablespoons instant coffee crystals
2 tablespoons Splenda Granular sweetener
1 1.4-ounce package sugar-free, Fat-free instant chocolate fudge pudding mix
2 cups Homemade Whipped Cream (page 190)
3 Nabisco Famous Chocolate Wafer cookies, coarsely crushed

1. In a medium mixing bowl, whisk together the milk, coffee crystals, and Splenda until coffee is dissolved completely.
2. Add the pudding mix and whisk until blended. Using a rubber spatula, gently stir in the Homemade Whipped Cream until thoroughly blended with the pudding mixture.
3. To serve, divide mousse among six dessert bowls and refrigerate until serving time. Just before serving, sprinkle each portion with some of the crushed chocolate wafers.

• APPROXIMATE NUTRITIONAL CONTENT •
Calories: 331, Protein: 4g, Net Carbs: 11g, Fat: 31g, Cholesterol: 112mg, Sodium: 288mg

triple-chocolate pudding

ESTIMATED PREPARATION TIME: 2 minutes (plus at least 2 hours cooling time)
COOK TIME: 3 minutes • **SERVINGS:** 4 (about $1/2$ cup per serving)

HOMEMADE CHOCOLATE PUDDING brings back memories of my mother's kitchen and the giant bowl she made pudding in for our large family. Waiting all day while it cooled and set was agony! This version is much quicker to set, thanks to the low-carb thickener (and a smaller bowl). To avoid a gummy texture, I combined the traditional cornstarch with the thickener and also made use of the new low-carb milk now available. The result is a quicker-setting, rich-tasting pudding that will please your whole family.

$1/4$ cup Splenda Granular sweetener

1 tablespoon sugar

1 tablespoon Sugar Twin brown sugar substitute

1 tablespoon cornstarch

2 tablespoons unsweetened cocoa powder

1 tablespoon Expert Foods' ThickenThin Not/Starch

2 cups low-carb chocolate milk

$1\frac{1}{2}$ ounces sugar-free dark chocolate, chopped

1 teaspoon vanilla extract

1. In a medium saucepan, whisk together the Splenda, sugar, Sugar Twin, cornstarch, cocoa powder, and low-carb thickener. Turn on the heat to medium and whisk in the low-carb milk. Cook, whisking frequently, until mixture is slightly thickened, about 10 minutes.

2. Remove from the heat and whisk in the chopped chocolate and vanilla, until chocolate is melted and combined.

3. Pour pudding into 4 individual dessert bowls, or into 1 shallow, larger bowl (such as a 1-quart casserole). Cover lightly with plastic wrap and refrigerate at least 2 hours before serving.

• **APPROXIMATE NUTRITIONAL CONTENT** •
Calories: 131, Protein: 7g, Net Carbs: 6g, Fat: 6g, Cholesterol: 13mg, Sodium: 183mg

tiramisu

ESTIMATED PREPARATION TIME: 20 minutes (plus at least 4 hours chilling time)
COOK TIME: none • **SERVINGS:** 12

𝓛OOK OUT: THIS dessert can be addictive! Tiramisu is one of my all-time favorite desserts, and the fact that this version is low in carbs makes it even better.

¾ cup light cream
1 1-ounce package sugar-free, fat-free vanilla instant pudding mix
1 8-ounce tub mascarpone cheese, softened
1 cup Homemade Whipped Cream (page 190)
3 tablespoons Kahlúa
3 tablespoons water
½ teaspoon instant coffee crystals
1 3-ounce package split ladyfingers (12 whole ladyfingers)
2 teaspoons unsweetened cocoa powder, divided
¾ ounce sugar-free dark chocolate, chopped (about 2 tablespoons)

1. In a large mixing bowl, using an electric mixer, mix the light cream and pudding mix until well combined, scraping bowl occasionally. Add the mascarpone and beat until smooth. Whisk the Homemade Whipped Cream into the pudding mixture (it will be very thick); set aside.

2. In a 1-cup measuring cup for liquids, stir together the Kahlúa, water, and coffee crystals until the crystals dissolve completely. Pour half the mixture into a shallow dish. Working with 6 ladyfinger halves at a time, lay the ladyfingers in the mixture and flip to soak both sides with the liquid (there should be liquid left over). Place the ladyfingers into an 8-inch or 9-inch square casserole; soak another 6 ladyfinger halves in the liquid remaining in the pan, then place them next to the others in the casserole dish, to make a complete bottom layer.

3. Using a rubber spatula, carefully spread half the pudding mixture over the soaked ladyfingers, spreading to the edge of the casserole dish. Sprinkle with 1 teaspoon of the cocoa powder. Pour the remaining Kahlúa mixture into the shallow dish and repeat the layers, ending with the cocoa. To garnish, sprinkle the chopped chocolate over the top. Cover tiramisu with plastic wrap and refrigerate at least 4 hours. To serve, cut into 12 squares and lift out servings with a small spatula.

• APPROXIMATE NUTRITIONAL CONTENT •
Calories: 228, Protein: 3g, Net Carbs: 9g, Fat: 19g, Cholesterol: 65mg, Sodium: 74mg

raspberry-white chocolate trifle

• •

ESTIMATED PREPARATION TIME: 25 minutes (plus at least 2 hours chilling time)
COOK TIME: none • **SERVINGS:** 14

• •

GREAT FOR A crowd, this stunning layered dessert will satisfy all your guests, whether they're "low-carbing" or not!

2 cups low-carb whole milk
1 cup plus ¼ cup water
1 1.4-ounce package sugar-free, fat-free white chocolate instant pudding mix
3 tablespoons Chambord liqueur
¼ cup water
2 3-ounce packages split ladyfingers (24 whole ladyfingers)
3 half-pints fresh raspberries, washed and well drained (about 3 cups)
2 cups Homemade Whipped Cream (page 190)
2 tablespoons white chocolate chips, chopped, for garnish

1. Pour the whole milk and 1 cup water together in a large mixing bowl. Using an electric mixer, blend in the pudding mix until well combined, scraping bowl with a rubber spatula occasionally; set aside. In a measuring cup for liquids, combine the Chambord with the ¼ cup water; set aside.

2. *To assemble the trifle:* In an 8-inch round trifle dish or large, deep glass bowl, place 8 ladyfinger halves to form a bottom layer. Using a pastry brush, brush the surface of the ladyfingers with some of the Chambord mixture. Pour a quarter of the pudding mixture over the ladyfinger layer, then sprinkle it with ½ cup of raspberries.

3. Place 16 ladyfinger halves, flat side up, on a plate; brush the flat surfaces with the Chambord mixture. Carefully position the ladyfingers, rounded side facing out, around the edge of the trifle bowl, forming a ring shape. Then, make another layer of 8 ladyfinger halves on top of the pudding layer, brush with the Chambord mixture, top with another quarter of pudding mixture and sprinkle with a scant ¾ cup of raspberries. Repeat layers 2 more times, reserving some raspberries for garnish (you'll use up all the pudding mixture, ladyfingers, and Chambord mixture).

4. Spread the top with the Homemade Whipped Cream. Garnish by sprinkling the top with the white chocolate chips and reserved raspberries. Refrigerate at least 2 hours before serving.

• **APPROXIMATE NUTRITIONAL CONTENT** •
Calories: 209, Protein: 4g, Net Carbs: 14g, Fat: 15g, Cholesterol: 73mg, Sodium: 223mg

mixed berry sorbet
page 146

chocolate-raspberry tartlets
page 174

pumpkin bars
page 81

tiramisu

page 115

chocolate-dipped strawberries
page 148

no-bake orange cheesecake
page 184

raspberry–white chocolate trifle

page 116

jam palmiers
page 88

peanut butter ice-cream terrine with hot fudge
page 133

chocolate cream pie
page 53

mocha drop cookies
page 69

cinnamon truffles
page 100

fluffy peanut butter trifle

ESTIMATED PREPARATION TIME: 25 minutes (plus at least 4 hours chilling time)
COOK TIME: none • **SERVINGS:** 12

*M*Y HUSBAND'S COWORKER, Marc Meglio, is a big peanut butter fan, so I created this trifle for him. It's an unusual flavor for a trifle, but it works.

•

1 8-ounce package Neufchâtel cheese, softened
¾ cup Splenda Granular sweetener, divided
¼ cup low-carb whole milk
½ cup low-carb peanut butter
½ teaspoon vanilla extract
2½ cups whipping cream, whipped until stiff peaks form
1 14-ounce low-carb pound cake (such as Entenmann's), cut into 1-inch cubes
1 tablespoon unsweetened cocoa powder, for garnish
6 Russell Stover sugar-free peanut butter cups, chopped, for garnish

•

1. In a large mixing bowl, using an electric mixer, blend the Neufchâtel cheese, Splenda, milk, peanut butter, and vanilla until smooth, about 5 minutes. Scrape down the bowl with a rubber spatula. Using the spatula, gently stir in the whipped cream until combined.

2. *To assemble the trifle:* Place one-third of the cake cubes in the bottom of an 8-inch round trifle bowl or large, deep glass bowl. Top with one-third of the peanut butter cream mixture, and spread it with the rubber spatula (it's okay if it doesn't completely cover the cake cubes). Repeat layers of cake and cream two more times, ending with the cream mixture on top (you'll use up all the cake cubes and cream mixture).

3. Cover bowl with plastic wrap and refrigerate at least 4 hours. When ready to serve, remove plastic and garnish the trifle by sprinkling the top with the cocoa powder and the chopped peanut butter cups.

• **APPROXIMATE NUTRITIONAL CONTENT** •
Calories: 418, Protein: 8g, Net Carbs: 9g, Fat: 36g, Cholesterol: 127mg, Sodium: 152mg

milk chocolate–almond soufflé for two

ESTIMATED PREPARATION TIME: 15 minutes
COOK TIME: 25 minutes • **SERVINGS:** 2

DON'T BE AFRAID to make a soufflé—it's not at all difficult! I can say that because this is the first soufflé I ever made in my life! All along I'd thought that soufflés were best left to the pros at restaurants, but this one came out perfectly the very first time: warm, fluffy, and with a good blend of chocolate and almond flavors! This is perfect for an intimate Valentine's Day dinner. Put it in the oven when you sit down to eat your meal, and it will be finished baking when you're ready for dessert.

1/2 teaspoon unsalted butter

2 teaspoons sugar

2 teaspoons flour

2 tablespoons Splenda Granular sweetener

1/4 cup whipping cream

2 eggs, separated, at room temperature, yolks lightly beaten with a fork

1 3-ounce bar sugar-free milk chocolate, chopped

1/4 teaspoon vanilla extract

1/8 teaspoon almond extract

pinch of salt

1. Preheat the oven to 375°F. Coat the inside of a 2-cup, straight-sided, ovenproof bowl or ramekin with the butter. Sprinkle the sugar all over the inside of the ramekin; set aside.

2. In a small, heavy saucepan, whisk together the flour and Splenda until combined, then add the whipping cream and cook 2 minutes over medium heat, whisking frequently. Place about 1 tablespoon of the cream mixture into the egg yolks and stir with a fork until combined; pour the egg yolk mixture back into the cream mixture and whisk until blended. Turn off the heat and set aside.

3. Put the chopped chocolate in a microwavable bowl and microwave on LOW power for 2 minutes, or until melted (stop halfway through to stir and check to see if it's melted yet). Whisk the melted chocolate into the reserved egg custard mixture. Add the extracts and salt and whisk again to combine; set aside.

4. In a small mixing bowl, using an electric mixer, beat the egg whites on high speed until they form stiff peaks. Gently whisk the beaten egg whites into the chocolate mixture until combined, taking care not to overmix it and "deflate" the egg whites (some white streaks may still be present in the mixture, but that's okay). Pour the mixture into the prepared ramekin and bake for 25 minutes, or until the soufflé is puffed, has dry cracks on the surface, and the center does not jiggle when the soufflé is very gently shaken. Remove from the oven and serve immediately.

---

cook's note

If you'd rather make a plain chocolate version, eliminate the almond extract and increase the vanilla extract to ½ teaspoon. You could also use sugar-free dark chocolate in this recipe, for a richer chocolate flavor.

• **APPROXIMATE NUTRITIONAL CONTENT** •
Calories: 404, Protein: 10g, Net Carbs: 7.5g, Fat: 31g, Cholesterol: 256mg, Sodium: 210mg

rum-raisin bread pudding

ESTIMATED PREPARATION TIME: 15 minutes (plus at least ½ hour cooling time)
COOK TIME: 35 minutes • **SERVINGS:** 9

THIS RECIPE IS "comfort food" at its low-carb best—bread, raisins, nutmeg, vanilla, and rum flavors all combine to yield a decidedly "grown-up" bread pudding. Be sure to let the pudding cool to nearly room temperature before serving, as it improves the flavor (or make it early in the day and leave it on the counter until serving time). You really shouldn't skip the Rum Whipped Cream, as it contributes much of the rum flavor.

cooking spray
16 slices Atkins Country White Bread, crusts trimmed (slightly stale bread is best)
1½ cups low-carb 2% milk
½ cup Sugar Twin brown sugar substitute
2 eggs, beaten
1 tablespoon rum extract
¼ teaspoon vanilla extract
¼ cup raisins (unpacked), chopped
2 teaspoons sugar
2 cups Rum Whipped Cream (page 195) (optional)

1. Preheat the oven to 325°F. Coat a 1½-quart casserole dish with cooking spray; set aside. Cut the bread slices into ½-inch cubes; set aside.
2. In a large mixing bowl, whisk together the milk, Sugar Twin, eggs, and extracts. Add the bread cubes to the bowl. Using a wooden spoon, stir the mixture to coat the bread cubes thoroughly. Stir in the chopped raisins, then spoon the mixture into the prepared casserole dish. Sprinkle the top of the pudding with the sugar.
3. Bake for 35 minutes, or until lightly browned on the top. Remove from the oven and let cool at least 30 minutes before serving. Garnish each portion with a generous dollop of Rum Whipped Cream, if desired.

• APPROXIMATE NUTRITIONAL CONTENT •
Calories: 128, Protein: 11g, Net Carbs: 9g, Fat: 4g, Cholesterol: 51mg, Sodium: 185mg

frozen desserts

frozen ambrosia squares

A COOL AND refreshing dessert that's reminiscent of ambrosia salad.

for the crust:

5 large graham cracker rectangles, crushed (about ¾ cup crumbs)
2 tablespoons butter, melted

for the ice-cream layer:

½ gallon low-carb vanilla ice cream, softened
1 8-ounce can crushed pineapple, well drained
1 8-ounce can mandarin orange segments, drained and roughly chopped
2 tablespoons unsweetened coconut, toasted

for the cream layer:

1 cup Homemade Whipped Cream (page 190)
½ teaspoon coconut extract
2 tablespoons unsweetened coconut, toasted

1. *To make the crust:* In a small bowl, stir together the graham cracker crumbs and melted butter until all graham cracker crumbs are moistened. Press mixture into the bottom of a 9-inch square baking pan; set aside.

2. *To make the ice-cream layer:* In a large bowl, using a wooden spoon, stir together the softened ice cream with the pineapple, orange pieces, and coconut until well combined. Using a rubber spatula, spread the ice cream over the graham cracker layer, being careful not to disturb the graham cracker crumbs. Place the pan in the freezer for 2 hours, or until surface is firm (mixture may not be frozen through). While waiting for the ice-cream layer to harden, prepare the cream layer.

3. *To make the cream layer:* In a small bowl, whisk together the Homemade Whipped Cream and coconut extract. Refrigerate mixture until the ice-cream layer is ready, then spread the cream mixture over the ice-cream layer, smoothing out the top. Sprinkle the top with the toasted coconut, then put the dessert back in the refrigerator for at least 3 more hours, until frozen through.

4. To serve, remove dessert from the freezer and let sit out for 5 to 10 minutes to soften slightly. Cutting the portions will be easier if you dip the knife in hot water (then wipe it dry) frequently.

• APPROXIMATE NUTRITIONAL CONTENT •
Calories: 250, Protein: 3g, Net Carbs: 11g, Fat: 19g, Cholesterol: 52mg, Sodium: 86mg

cool crème de menthe torte

ESTIMATED PREPARATION TIME: 15 minutes (plus at least 3½ hours freezing time)
COOK TIME: 15 minutes • **SERVINGS:** 12

THIS IMPRESSIVE TORTE has three layers, yet it's a snap to prepare. Just be sure to allow sufficient time, as each layer is briefly frozen before the next one is added.

for the brownie layer:

cooking spray
1 8.5-ounce package Atkins Quick Quisine Fudge Brownie Mix
2 eggs
⅓ cup water
⅓ cup oil

for the mousse layer:

1 2.8-ounce package Nestlé milk chocolate mousse mix
⅔ cup low-carb whole milk
1½ tablespoons crème de menthe

for the cream layer:

1 cup whipping cream
2 tablespoons crème de menthe
green food coloring

6 Russell Stover sugar-free peppermint patty candies, cut in half

1. Preheat the oven to 350°F.

2. *To make the brownie layer:* Spray the bottom and sides of a 10-inch springform pan with cooking spray; set aside. In a small bowl, stir together the brownie mix with the eggs, water, and oil (do not follow package directions that call for just 1 egg). Using a rubber spatula, spread the brownie batter on the bottom of the springform pan to make an even, but thin layer. Bake for 15 minutes; remove from oven and let cool 10 minutes. Transfer pan to the freezer for ½ hour. While the brownie layer is in the freezer, prepare the mousse layer.

3. *To make the mousse layer:* In a medium bowl, using an electric mixer on medium speed, blend the mousse mix with the milk and crème de menthe for 1 minute.

Scrape bowl well with a rubber spatula; increase mixer speed to medium-high and beat another 2 minutes, then scrape bowl again. Continue to beat for 3 more minutes on medium-high speed, until mousse turns lighter in color and becomes fluffy. Remove the brownie layer from the freezer. Using a rubber spatula, spread the mousse mixture over the brownie layer, making a smooth, even layer. Return pan to freezer for 1 hour. Toward the end of the 1-hour freezing time, prepare the cream layer.

4. *To make the cream layer:* In a medium mixing bowl, using an electric mixer on medium-high speed, whip the cream and crème de menthe until light and fluffy, about 4 minutes. Add a few drops of green food coloring to tint it light green, and whip again to blend, adding more food coloring as necessary to achieve the desired shade of green. Remove the torte from the freezer and spread the cream over the mousse layer, spreading it to the edges smoothly with a rubber spatula. Place the peppermint patty halves, cut side down, in an even circle pattern around the top of the torte so that each serving will get one piece of patty as a garnish (mark the servings first with a long knife, if you wish). Return finished torte to the freezer for at least 2 hours before serving.

5. To serve, remove dessert from the freezer and let sit out for 5 minutes to soften slightly. Run a sharp knife around the inside edge of the pan to loosen the torte, then remove the ring from the pan. Cutting the portions will be easier if you dip the knife in hot water frequently.

• APPROXIMATE NUTRITIONAL CONTENT •
Calories: 186, Protein: 3g, Net Carbs: 13g, Fat: 9g, Cholesterol: 37mg, Sodium: 109mg

chocolate ice-cream sundae "cake"

ESTIMATED PREPARATION TIME: 15 minutes (plus at least 4 hours freezing time)
COOK TIME: none • **SERVINGS:** 16

THIS DESSERT HAS all the typical ice-cream sundae ingredients—ice cream, strawberry topping, and peanuts—and is served with Chocolate Glaze and Homemade Whipped Cream. It's a nice alternative to a regular cake for a summertime birthday celebration.

cooking spray
4 large chocolate graham cracker rectangles
½ gallon low-carb chocolate ice cream, softened
1 cup Smucker's sugar-free, "light" strawberry preserves, whisked to remove lumps
½ cup cocktail peanuts, chopped
2 recipes Chocolate Glaze (page 198)
2 cups Homemade Whipped Cream (optional garnish) (page 190)

1. Spray an 8-inch or 9-inch square baking pan with cooking spray. Place the graham crackers in the bottom of the pan to make a crust, breaking them as needed to completely cover the bottom of the pan (if a few overlap, that's okay).

2. Using a rubber spatula, carefully spread half the softened ice cream over the graham crackers. Pour whisked preserves over the ice-cream layer and spread with the spatula all the way to the edges. Top with the remaining ice cream, carefully spreading it to the edges. Sprinkle the top with the peanuts and freeze the "cake" at least 4 hours, or until firm.

3. Prepare the Chocolate Glaze and Homemade Whipped Cream before serving (you can warm the glaze in the microwave just prior to serving, if desired). Pass both when serving the "cake." To serve, remove the "cake" from the freezer and let it sit out for 5 to 10 minutes to soften slightly. Cutting the portions will be easier if you dip the knife in hot water (then wipe it dry) frequently.

• **EACH SERVING (WITH GLAZE BUT NOT WHIPPED CREAM) CONTAINS APPROXIMATELY** •
Calories: 240, Protein: 4g, Net Carbs: 11g, Fat: 18g, Cholesterol: 30mg, Sodium: 81mg

chocolate-chunk baked alaska

ESTIMATED PREPARATION TIME: 20 minutes (plus at least 6 hours freezing time)
COOK TIME: 30 minutes • **SERVINGS:** 12

THIS IS THE dish you'll want to make when your aim is to impress. A tall mound of golden-tipped meringue hides the chocolate-studded ice cream layer and moist chocolate cake. This stunning dessert contains more carbs than other recipes in this book, but it still is much lower in carbs than the traditional version.

for the cake:
cooking spray
1 8-ounce package Sweet'N Low no-added-sugar chocolate cake mix
¾ cup water
¼ teaspoon vanilla extract
1 tablespoon Atkins Sugar-Free Chocolate Syrup

for the ice-cream filling:
½ gallon low-carb vanilla ice cream, softened
2 3-ounce bars sugar-free milk chocolate, chopped

for the meringue:
6 egg whites, room temperature
⅛ teaspoon cream of tartar
2 tablespoons sugar
2 tablespoons Splenda Granular sweetener

1. Preheat the oven to 350°F. Spray an 8-inch round cake pan with cooking spray; set aside.
2. *To make the cake:* In a medium mixing bowl, combine the water, vanilla, and chocolate syrup. Add the cake mix and blend with an electric mixer on low speed, increasing to medium-high speed, until well blended and slightly fluffy, about 4 minutes. Pour batter into prepared pan and bake for 25 minutes, or until top springs back when touched lightly in the center.
3. Remove from the oven and let cool 10 minutes. Turn cake out onto a cooling rack and cool completely. Using a serrated knife, trim off the round top of the cake;

discard the trimmings. Place the cake into a 9-inch pie plate and freeze until needed.

4. *To make the filling:* In a medium mixing bowl, using a wooden spoon, stir together the softened ice cream and chopped chocolate until well combined. Spray a 2½-quart metal or glass bowl with cooking spray (the top edge of the bowl should be 8 inches across). Using a wooden spoon, transfer the ice cream to the prepared bowl, packing it down and smoothing the top. Cover with plastic wrap and freeze at least 4 hours, or until firm.

5. When firm, unmold the ice cream from the bowl by dipping the bowl into a sink full of hot water for about 15 seconds (be careful not to let water get into the bowl). Run a long knife carefully around the inside edge of the bowl to help the ice cream release from the bowl, then flip it over onto the frozen cake layer. If ice cream does not release, re-dip it and try again. Once the ice cream mound is in place on the cake layer, cover it lightly with plastic wrap and place it in the freezer for another 2 hours, or until firm.

6. Just prior to serving, preheat the oven to 450°F.

7. *To make the meringue:* In a medium mixing bowl, using an electric mixer on medium-high speed, beat the egg whites with the cream of tartar until foamy. Increase the speed to high and add the sugar, 1 tablespoon at a time, until egg whites are glossy. Add the Splenda and beat again until egg whites are stiff but not dry.

8. Remove the ice cream and cake layers from the freezer. Working quickly, scoop the meringue onto the ice cream, covering the entire mound, and making sure that some meringue touches the edge of the pie plate all around (or it will shrink when baked). Swirl the meringue decoratively with the back of a spoon. Bake for about 4 minutes, or until the tips of the meringue are golden brown. Remove from the oven and serve immediately. Cutting the portions will be easier if you dip the knife in hot water (then wipe it dry) frequently.

• **APPROXIMATE NUTRITIONAL CONTENT** •
Calories: 320, Protein: 7g, Net Carbs: 17g, Fat: 18g, Cholesterol: 33mg, Sodium: 83mg

fried butter pecan ice cream

ESTIMATED PREPARATION TIME: 15 minutes (plus at least 4 hours freezing time)
COOK TIME: 2 minutes • **SERVINGS:** 5

$\mathcal{I}$ FIRST HAD fried ice cream in San Francisco while traveling with my family, when I was a child. I remember it well because my sisters and I all loved it immediately—the contrast between the hot, crunchy coating and cool, creamy ice cream was so unique and delicious! The novelty of the dessert made such a big impression on us that we begged our parents to let us go back to that same restaurant for dessert nearly every night of our vacation. This low-carb adaptation delivers a lot of pecan flavor. If you prefer a different flavor combination, feel free to change the ice cream, nuts, or even add some cinnamon to the recipe—it will still turn out great.

1 pint Atkins Endulge Butter-Pecan Ice Cream

for the coating:
8 Murray's sugar-free, ring-shaped shortbread cookies, crushed
$\frac{1}{3}$ cup pecans, finely chopped
$\frac{1}{4}$ cup unsweetened coconut
1 tablespoon Splenda Granular sweetener
1 egg, slightly beaten

Peanut oil for frying

1. Using an ice cream scoop, form the ice cream into 5 ice-cream balls. Place the balls on a plate lined with waxed paper or parchment and freeze until very firm, at least 2 hours.
2. *To make the coating:* In a small bowl, stir together the shortbread crumbs, pecans, coconut, and Splenda until combined; set aside.
3. When ice-cream balls are frozen, remove them from the freezer and roll each in the coating mixture. Dip the balls into the beaten egg, covering all sides, and then roll the balls in the coating mixture again, covering all sides thoroughly. Return the balls to the freezer for at least 2 more hours, or until very firm.
4. Just before serving, heat 2 inches of peanut oil in a heavy, deep saucepan, deep fryer or heavy skillet, until oil reaches 375°F. Fry the ice-cream balls, one at a time, for about 20 seconds, until the coating is nicely browned (watch carefully,

because it can burn quickly). Remove the balls from the oil with a slotted spoon, letting the oil drain off for a moment. Serve immediately.

• **APPROXIMATE NUTRITIONAL CONTENT** •
Calories: 270, Protein: 4g, Net Carbs: 7g, Fat: 24g, Cholesterol: 75mg, Sodium: 74mg

maple-pecan ice-cream pie

ESTIMATED PREPARATION TIME: 10 minutes (plus at least 5 hours freezing time)
COOK TIME: none • **SERVINGS:** 10

*W*HAT'S NOT TO like? A crunchy crust, creamy ice cream, and luscious maple and pecan flavors...plus, it's really easy!

2½ pints Atkins Endulge Butter Pecan Ice Cream, softened
2 tablespoons sugar-free maple syrup
2 Russell Stover Sugar Free Pecan Delights candies, finely chopped

1 recipe Nutty Graham Crust, made with pecans, baked in a 9-inch pie plate, and cooled (page 61)

1. In a medium mixing bowl, stir together the softened ice cream and the maple syrup until well combined and smooth. Transfer the ice-cream mixture to the prepared crust, smoothing the top with a rubber spatula.

2. Sprinkle the top of the pie with the chopped candies. Place pie in the freezer for 5 hours (or overnight) until frozen throughout.

3. To serve, remove the pie from the freezer and let it sit out for 5 minutes to soften slightly. Cutting the portions will be easier if you dip the knife in hot water frequently.

• APPROXIMATE NUTRITIONAL CONTENT •
Calories: 312, Protein: 3g, Net Carbs: 12g, Fat: 26g, Cholesterol: 52mg, Sodium: 71mg

peanut butter ice-cream terrine with hot fudge

Prep time: 15 minutes (plus at least 6 hours freezing time)
COOK TIME: none • **SERVINGS:** 10

A TERRINE IS a layered, loaf-shaped dish often associated with savory foods and appetizers. I think you'll prefer this version, which features a crunchy layer of crushed cookies, peanuts, and peanut butter, sandwiched between layers of chocolate–peanut butter swirl ice cream. If you're feeling adventurous, you could alter the cookies and ice-cream flavors, but use the same basic technique to create your own unique ice cream terrine.

cooking spray
6 Murray's sugar-free peanut butter cookies, finely crushed, divided
$\frac{1}{4}$ cup cocktail peanuts, chopped, divided
2 pints Atkins Endulge Chocolate Peanut Butter Swirl Ice Cream, softened
$\frac{1}{2}$ cup low-carb peanut butter
2 recipes Low-Carb Hot Fudge (page 197)

1. Line an 8½-by-3½-inch loaf pan with plastic wrap, leaving a 4-inch overhang of wrap on each long side of the pan. Coat the plastic wrap with cooking spray. Place half of cookie crumbs in bottom of pan; shake pan to evenly distribute the crumbs. Sprinkle crumbs with half the chopped peanuts.

2. Using a rubber spatula, carefully spread 1 quart of the softened ice cream over the nut and crumb layer. Spread the peanut butter over the ice cream, then sprinkle with the remaining cookie crumbs and peanuts. Top with the second pint of ice cream and spread smooth. Cover the pan with plastic wrap and freeze at least 6 hours, or until frozen through.

3. To serve, remove terrine from the freezer and let it sit out for 5 to 10 minutes to soften. Using the plastic wrap, lift the terrine from the pan and invert it onto a cutting board. Cut the terrine into 10 slices (it will be easier if you dip the knife in hot water, then wipe it dry between slices). Transfer slices to individual dessert plates, then drizzle each portion with the Low-Carb Hot Fudge.

• **APPROXIMATE NUTRITIONAL CONTENT** •
Calories: 390, Protein: 8g, Net Carbs: 7.5g, Fat: 31g, Cholesterol: 49mg, Sodium: 277mg

chocolate chip cookie ice-cream pie

ESTIMATED PREPARATION TIME: 10 minutes (plus at least 4$\frac{1}{2}$ hours cooling/freezing time)
COOK TIME: 15 minutes • **SERVINGS:** 10

THIS FAMILY-PLEASING dessert uses low-carb chocolate chip cookie mix for the crust, so it's easy on the cook. Topped with low-carb ice cream mixed with chocolate chunks and a sprinkle of nuts, it has all the traditional chocolate chip cookie tastes, plus the cool creaminess of ice cream.

for the crust:
cooking spray
1 8-ounce package Atkins Quick Quisine Chocolate Chip Cookie Mix
3 tablespoons butter, softened
1 egg
1 tablespoon water

1 pint low-carb chocolate or vanilla ice cream, softened
1 3-ounce bar sugar-free dark chocolate, chopped
$\frac{1}{4}$ cup walnuts or pecans, chopped

1. Preheat oven to 350°F.
2. *To make the crust:* Spray a 9-inch or 10-inch pie plate with cooking spray (a springform pan would also work well). In a medium mixing bowl, prepare the cookie mix according to package directions using the butter, egg, and water. Using a rubber spatula, spread the dough into the bottom of the prepared pie plate and bake for 12 to 15 minutes, until set but not browned. Cool crust completely (about ½ hour).
3. In a small mixing bowl, stir together the softened ice cream and the chopped chocolate; spread over the cooled cookie crust using a rubber spatula. Sprinkle with the chopped nuts and freeze the pie for at least 4 hours, until firm.
4. To serve, remove the pie from the freezer and let it sit out for 5 to 10 minutes to soften slightly. Cutting the portions will be easier if you dip the knife in hot water (then wipe it dry) frequently.

• **APPROXIMATE NUTRITIONAL CONTENT** •
Calories: 229, Protein: 6g, Net Carbs: 9g, Fat: 13g, Cholesterol: 41mg, Sodium: 94mg

mocha waffle sundaes

ESTIMATED PREPARATION TIME: 15 minutes (plus at least 1 hour freezing time)
COOK TIME: none (make the waffles ahead of time) • **SERVINGS:** 4

THIS SPECIAL DESSERT is fit for company. Making the waffles ahead of time ensures this will be a snap to put together. You could even set up a "make your own waffle sundae" station and let your guests help themselves. If your carb budget allows it, feel free to top the sundaes with Low-Carb Hot Fudge (page 97) as well.

•

4 individual ½-cup portions Atkins Endulge Chocolate Ice Cream, softened (keep original containers)
2 teaspoons instant coffee crystals, divided
4 premade Chocolate Belgian Waffles (page 98), thawed, if previously frozen
1 cup Homemade Whipped Cream (page 190)
4 teaspoons mini semi-sweet chocolate chips

•

1. Working with one portion of ice cream at a time, stir together the softened ice cream and ½ teaspoon of the coffee crystals in a small bowl. When well mixed, spoon the ice cream back into the plastic cup it came in, re-cover it with the lid, and return to the freezer for at least 1 hour, until it's refrozen. Repeat with the remaining 3 portions of ice cream and the remaining coffee crystals.

2. When all ice cream portions are refrozen, and you're ready to serve the dessert, assemble the sundaes: Remove ice-cream portions from the freezer and let them sit out for 5 minutes to soften slightly. Place waffles on individual dessert dishes. Run a butter knife around the inside edge of each ice-cream portion, then invert them over the waffles (you may need to help them along a bit with a spoon).

3. Top each portion with ¼ cup of Homemade Whipped Cream, and garnish each sundae by sprinkling with 1 teaspoon mini chocolate chips. Serve immediately.

• APPROXIMATE NUTRITIONAL CONTENT •
Calories: 455, Protein: 11g, Net Carbs: 9g, Fat: 28g, Cholesterol: 141mg, Sodium: 207mg

cherry waffle sundaes

ESTIMATED PREPARATION TIME: 5 minutes
COOK TIME: none (pre-make the waffles) • **SERVINGS:** 4

AN EASY DESSERT featuring cherries and chocolate, a favorite flavor combination.

4 premade Chocolate Belgian Waffles (page 98), thawed, if previously frozen
4 individual ½-cup portions Atkins Endulge Vanilla Ice Cream, softened slightly
12 tablespoons canned No-Sugar-Added Cherry Pie Filling (not "Light" filling), divided

1. Place each waffle on a microwavable dessert plate. Working with one plate at a time, microwave the waffle for 15 seconds on MEDIUM power.
2. Immediately top the waffle with a ½-cup portion of the ice cream (invert the cup over the waffle, and help the ice cream out with a spoon). Top the ice cream with 3 tablespoons of the pie filling. Repeat with the remaining waffles, ice cream, and pie filling. Serve immediately.

• **APPROXIMATE NUTRITIONAL CONTENT** •
Calories: 247, Protein: 11g, Net Carbs: 14g, Fat: 5g, Cholesterol: 93mg, Sodium: 198mg

easy chocolate–vanilla ice–cream sandwiches

. . . .

ESTIMATED PREPARATION TIME: 5 minutes (plus at least 2 hours freezing time)
COOK TIME: none • **SERVINGS:** 4

. . . .

WHEN YOU'RE DESPERATE for an ice–cream treat on a hot summer's day, it'd be handy to have a few of these ready and waiting in your freezer.

•

8 Nabisco Famous Chocolate Wafer cookies
1 cup Atkins Endulge Vanilla Fudge Swirl Ice Cream, softened slightly, divided
4 teaspoons chocolate jimmies (or favorite ice-cream sprinkles), divided

•

1. Using a ¼-cup measure, scoop the softened ice cream and level off the measuring cup with a butter knife. Make one sandwich at a time by inverting the measuring cup of ice cream onto one of the cookies, then topping with another cookie and pressing them together gently, to form the sandwich.
2. Place 1 teaspoon of the jimmies on a small plate and roll the edges of the sandwich in the jimmies for a garnish. Wrap the sandwich in plastic wrap and place in the freezer.
3. Repeat with remaining ice cream, cookies, and jimmies to make 4 sandwiches. Let sandwiches freeze at least 2 hours, until firm, before serving.

• APPROXIMATE NUTRITIONAL CONTENT •
Calories: 146, Protein: 2g, Net Carbs: 15g, Fat: 8g, Cholesterol: 20mg, Sodium: 107mg

jack's rich chocolate shake

ESTIMATED PREPARATION TIME: 5 minutes
COOK TIME: none • **SERVINGS:** 2

*M*Y SON, JACK, loves milkshakes, so one day we created this simple shake to satisfy his craving on a warm summer's afternoon. It's equally good in the vanilla version (see below).

¾ cup low-carb chocolate milk
1½ cups low-carb chocolate ice cream
¼ teaspoon vanilla extract

1. Add ingredients to blender in the order listed. Blend on low speed for about 1 minute, then increase to high speed until shake is smooth, but still thick.
2. Pour into two glasses and serve immediately with straws.

• **EACH (1-CUP) SERVING CONTAINS APPROXIMATELY** •
Calories: 234, Protein: 8g, Net Carbs: 7g, Fat: 17g, Cholesterol: 47mg, Sodium: 206mg

variation

VERY VANILLA SHAKE

*F*OR A VANILLA shake, substitute these ingredients, then follow the directions above:

¾ cup low-carb 2% milk
1½ cups low-carb vanilla ice cream
½ teaspoon vanilla extract

• **EACH (1-CUP) SERVING CONTAINS APPROXIMATELY** •
Calories: 235, Protein: 8g, Net Carbs: 7.5g, Fat: 15g, Cholesterol: 45mg, Sodium: 116mg

root beer float

THIS WILL TAKE you back to your childhood! This is so easy, there's no reason not to indulge, especially during the hot summer months. For other soda–ice cream combinations, see the variations below.

1 12-ounce can chilled diet root beer
1 cup low-carb vanilla ice cream, softened slightly, divided

1. Divide the root beer between two 12-ounce glasses or mugs (chill the glasses briefly in the freezer to make them frosty beforehand, if you wish).
2. Top each portion with a half-cup scoop of the softened ice cream. Serve immediately, with a spoon and a straw.

• APPROXIMATE NUTRITIONAL CONTENT •
Calories: 130, Protein: 2g, Net Carbs: 4g, Fat: 9g, Cholesterol: 25mg, Sodium: 25mg

variations

PURPLE COW: Use diet grape soda instead of the root beer.
CREAM SODA CHILLER: Use diet cream soda instead of the root beer.
COKE FLOAT: Use Diet Coke (or your favorite diet cola) instead of the root beer.

basic homemade vanilla ice cream

ESTIMATED PREPARATION TIME: 5 minutes (plus at least 1 hour chilling time
and about 30 minutes processing time) • **COOK TIME:** none • **SERVINGS:** 8 (½ cup each)

VANILLA ICE CREAM is the perfect accompaniment to many other desserts, in which case store-bought ice cream will do. However, if you want a soft, homemade version, this is your recipe. If you prefer flecks of vanilla bean in your ice cream, decrease the vanilla extract to 1 teaspoon, and add a half-teaspoon of vanilla bean paste, which is available from baking supply catalogs and at specialty stores. Try the mix-in ideas, below, to "customize" your dessert.

2 cups heavy cream
½ cup low-carb whole milk
½ cup light cream
¾ cup Splenda Granular sweetener
2 tablespoons sugar
1½ teaspoons vanilla extract

1. In a quart-sized measuring cup for liquids, or a medium mixing bowl, whisk together all ingredients until the sugar is completely dissolved. Place a piece of plastic wrap directly on the surface of the mixture. Refrigerate mixture at least 1 hour.
2. Process the chilled ice-cream mixture (the ice-cream "base") in your ice-cream maker, according to manufacturer's directions. If desired, stir in additional "mix-in" ingredients and serve immediately, or freeze an additional two hours for a firmer consistency.

• APPROXIMATE NUTRITIONAL CONTENT •
Calories: 256, Protein: 2g, Net Carbs: 5.5g, Fat: 25g, Cholesterol: 94mg, Sodium: 42mg

ice cream "mix-in" ideas

Crumbled low-carb cookies
Chopped low-carb candies or candy-bars (toffee or peppermint candies
are especially good)
Chopped toasted nuts
Fresh or frozen berries (strawberries should be sliced or chopped)

frozen hot chocolate

ESTIMATED PREPARATION TIME: 15 minutes (plus at least 1 hour chilling time and about 30 minutes processing time) • **COOK TIME:** none • **SERVINGS:** 8 (½ cup each)

THIS IS AN easy way to make a good approximation of chocolate soft-serve ice cream (which I happen to love but usually abstain from, these days). The basic idea here is to make a rich batch of easy hot chocolate using mix, then freeze it to just the right consistency. Spooning it into mugs and topping with Homemade Whipped Cream is a novel way to enjoy this treat any time of year.

2 cups heavy cream
½ cup low-carb whole milk
½ cup light cream
Half a 3-ounce bar sugar-free dark chocolate, finely chopped
2 0.55-ounce packets no-sugar-added instant cocoa mix (such as Swiss Miss)
1 tablespoon sugar
½ teaspoon vanilla extract
Homemade Whipped Cream (page 190), optional

1. In a medium, heavy saucepan, over medium heat, whisk together the heavy cream, low-carb milk, and light cream. Add the chopped chocolate and heat, whisking constantly, until the chocolate is blended well. Add both envelopes of cocoa mix and whisk until blended, about 3 minutes. Remove from heat and whisk in sugar and vanilla until sugar is completely dissolved.

2. Place a piece of plastic wrap directly on the surface of the mixture. Refrigerate mixture at least 1 hour.

3. Process the chilled ice-cream mixture (the ice-cream "base") in your ice-cream maker, according to manufacturer's directions, until it achieves soft-serve consistency. Spoon into mugs or bowls, and top with Homemade Whipped Cream, if desired.

• APPROXIMATE NUTRITIONAL CONTENT •
Calories: 283, Protein: 4g, Net Carbs: 5.5g, Fat: 27g, Cholesterol: 94mg, Sodium: 84mg

coconut ice cream

ESTIMATED PREPARATION TIME: 15 minutes (plus at least 1 hour chilling time and about 30 minutes processing time) • **COOK TIME:** none • **SERVINGS:** 8 (¹/₂ cup each)

THIS IS A super-creamy dessert that's great on its own, and is even better when drizzled with a little Low-Carb Hot Fudge (page 197). The toasted coconut Provides some nice texture to this ice cream, but if you prefer a smooth ice cream, feel free to omit it and add a little extra coconut extract (¹/₈–¹/₄ teaspoon).

1³/₄ cups heavy cream
1 cup low-carb whole milk
¹/₄ cup unsweetened coconut milk
1 teaspoon coconut extract
¹/₄ teaspoon vanilla extract
³/₄ cup Splenda Granular sweetener
2 tablespoons sugar
¹/₄ cup unsweetened coconut, toasted

1. In a quart-sized measuring cup for liquids, or a medium mixing bowl, whisk together the heavy cream, low-carb whole milk, coconut milk, and extracts. Stir in the Splenda and sugar with a wooden spoon, until sugar is completely dissolved. Place a piece of plastic wrap directly on the surface of the mixture. Refrigerate mixture at least 1 hour.

2. Process the chilled ice-cream mixture (the ice-cream "base") in your ice-cream maker, according to manufacturer's directions. If desired, stir in the toasted coconut. Serve immediately, or freeze an additional two hours for a firmer consistency.

• APPROXIMATE NUTRITIONAL CONTENT •
Calories: 236, Protein: 3g, Net Carbs: 5g, Fat: 23g, Cholesterol: 76mg, Sodium: 48mg

caramel ice cream

*U*TILIZING SUGAR-FREE chocolate-covered caramel candies makes this ice cream a snap to prepare. Its flavor is rich, but not overwhelming, and the smooth ice-cream texture is accented by a few chewy chunks of caramel candy. This is one of my family's favorites on its own, but it would also be fabulous served alongside a small portion of sautéed apple slices.

2 cups heavy cream

⅔ cup Sugar Twin brown sugar substitute

2 tablespoons light brown sugar

½ cup low-carb whole milk

½ cup light cream

1 teaspoon vanilla extract

1 3.5-ounce package Russell Stover sugar-free chocolate-covered caramels, (about 10 candies), quartered, divided

1. In a quart-sized measuring cup for liquids, or medium mixing bowl, whisk together the heavy cream, Sugar Twin, and brown sugar, until the sugar is completely dissolved. Add the low-carb milk, light cream, and vanilla, and whisk until blended; set aside.

2. In a small saucepan, over low heat, partially melt two-thirds of the caramel candies, about 1 minute, stirring with a wooden spoon (set aside remaining one-third of chopped candies to add to the ice cream at the end of processing). Add 2 tablespoons of the cream mixture to the pan and stir to blend with the caramels. Remove from heat when there are still some chunks of caramel left (it should not be completely melted). Scrape the caramel mixture into the cream mixture and stir to combine. Place a piece of plastic wrap directly on the surface of the cream mixture. Refrigerate mixture at least 1 hour.

3. Process the chilled ice-cream mixture (the ice-cream "base") in your ice-cream maker, according to manufacturer's directions. This ice cream benefits from additional freezing time, but it can be eaten immediately if you just can't wait!

• **APPROXIMATE NUTRITIONAL CONTENT** •

Calories: 309, Protein: 3g, Net Carbs: 6g, Fat: 29g, Cholesterol: 94mg, Sodium: 61mg

deep, dark chocolate ice cream

ESTIMATED PREPARATION TIME: 20 minutes (plus at least 4 hours chilling time
and about 30 minutes processing time) • **COOK TIME:** none • **SERVINGS:** 8 (½ cup each)

*U*NLIKE THE OTHER ice creams in this book, this one utilizes a cooked base (though it contains no eggs, unlike traditional cooked ice-cream bases). The result of cooking the base is that the ice cream is smoother and more like a premium ice cream than a soft-serve-type product.

2 cups heavy cream

3 1-ounce squares unsweetened baking chocolate, chopped

2 tablespoons sugar

1 3-ounce bar sugar-free bittersweet chocolate, chopped

½ cup low-carb whole milk

½ cup light cream

½ cup Splenda Granular sweetener

½ teaspoon vanilla extract

1. In a medium, heavy saucepan, over medium-low heat, whisk the cream, unsweetened chocolate, sugar, and sugar-free chocolate constantly, until the mixture is smooth. Continue to whisk constantly until mixture comes to a simmer, about 10 minutes. (No chocolate bits should remain; chocolate should be completely melted.)

2. Remove from heat and whisk in the remaining ingredients. Place a piece of plastic wrap directly on the surface of the mixture. Refrigerate mixture at least 4 hours.

3. Process the chilled ice-cream mixture (the ice-cream "base") in your ice-cream maker, according to manufacturer's directions. Serve immediately, or freeze another 2 hours for a firmer consistency.

• APPROXIMATE NUTRITIONAL CONTENT •
Calories: 353, Protein: 4g, Net Carbs: 8g, Fat: 35g, Cholesterol: 94mg, Sodium: 43mg

lemon-lime yogurt slush

ESTIMATED PREPARATION TIME: 10 minutes (plus at least 2 hours chilling time and about 20 minutes processing time) • **COOK TIME:** none • **SERVINGS:** 10 ($\frac{1}{2}$ cup each)

THIS REFRESHING FROZEN treat is like a "grown-up" version of the snow cones I used to get at parades and fairs. Because it contains yogurt, it's a tad creamier, yet it still retains a crystallized texture. No matter what you call it, I think you'll agree that it's particularly refreshing.

3 cups water
2 4-ounce cups low-carb vanilla yogurt
$\frac{1}{2}$ cup fresh lemon juice
$\frac{1}{4}$ cup fresh lime juice
2 tablespoons sugar
1 tablespoon grated lime peel
1 "tub" sugar-free lemonade mix (such as Crystal Light)

1. Whisk together all ingredients in a pitcher until blended. Cover pitcher with plastic wrap and chill at least 2 hours.
2. Process the chilled mixture in an ice-cream maker, according to manufacturer's directions (in my machine, this mixture froze faster than ice cream does, so watch your machine carefully). Serve immediately, then transfer any leftovers to a plastic container with a lid and store in the freezer. (The mixture will freeze very hard in the freezer. To serve leftovers, let it sit out for 20 minutes before scooping.)

• **APPROXIMATE NUTRITIONAL CONTENT** •
Calories: 29, Protein: 1g, Net Carbs: 6g, Fat: 1g, Cholesterol: 2mg, Sodium: 6mg

mixed berry sorbet

BURSTING WITH BERRY flavor, this sorbet tastes just like what you'd get at a fancy restaurant—minus the hefty price tag. This is a nice recipe to make for company; serve it with a low-carb cookie for a light dessert. If you'd like, you can just use one type of berry, such as strawberries or raspberries. Do not be tempted to remove the sugar from the recipe and use just Splenda; the sorbet needs the sugar for proper crystallization and "real" flavor.

2 12-ounce bags frozen mixed berries, thawed

2 cups water

½ cup Splenda Granular sweetener

¼ cup sugar

1. Add all ingredients to a blender and process about 1 minute, until pureed.
2. Strain mixture in batches, through a sieve, over a medium mixing bowl, to remove the seeds and pulp. Press the mixture with the back of a wooden spoon to help force it through the sieve, and scoop out the seeds every so often. This is the time-consuming part of the recipe; it may take 10 minutes for all the liquid to drip through the sieve. You should have 5 cups of liquid.
3. Cover the bowl with plastic wrap and refrigerate at least 2 hours.
4. Process the sorbet liquid in an ice-cream maker, according to manufacturer's directions. Transfer the soft sorbet to a plastic container with a lid, then freeze until very firm, at least 4 hours, before serving.

• APPROXIMATE NUTRITIONAL CONTENT •
Calories: 49, Protein: 0g, Net Carbs: 11g, Fat: 0g, Cholesterol: 0mg, Sodium: 0mg

fruit desserts

chocolate-dipped strawberries

ESTIMATED PREPARATION TIME: 10 minutes (plus 1 hour cooling time)
COOK TIME: 3 minutes • **SERVINGS:** 4

THIS IS A great way to showcase beautiful strawberries, and they're easy to make—even the kids can help! If you're lucky enough to find some nice berries during the winter months, buy them for this recipe; you'll be amazed at how refreshing they can be to a winter-weary palate. They make a lovely Valentine's Day dessert, too!

1 3-ounce bar sugar-free dark chocolate, chopped
1 tablespoon shortening
12 large strawberries, with green caps attached (and stems, if possible), washed and left
on paper towels to air-dry

1. In a small microwavable bowl, combine the chopped chocolate with the shortening. Microwave on MEDIUM power for 1 minute, then stir. Continue to microwave on MEDIUM for 1 to 2 minutes more, stopping every 30 seconds to stir and check to see if the chocolate is melted (it will not appear to be melted, so you'll need to stir it to check). Once the chocolate has melted, stir thoroughly to incorporate the shortening.
2. Working quickly, with one strawberry at a time, hold the berry by the cap (or stem) firmly but gently; dip the berry into the melted chocolate mixture so that the chocolate reaches about three-fourths of the way up the strawberry. Turn the berry so that all sides are equally coated with chocolate. Lift the berry out of the chocolate and gently scrape the bottom of the berry along the rim of the bowl to remove excess chocolate. Place the berry on waxed paper with the tip pointing down at a 45-degree angle (don't place the berry flat on its side). Repeat with remaining berries and chocolate.
3. Let the coated berries sit on the counter for 1 hour, until the chocolate cools and dries. Transfer the berries to the refrigerator until serving time. These berries are best eaten the day they're prepared.

• EACH SERVING (3 BERRIES) CONTAINS APPROXIMATELY •
Calories: 156, Protein: 2g, Net Carbs: 10g, Fat: 11g, Cholesterol: 0mg, Sodium: 2mg

ingredient note

If the berries you have are not very large, use 16 medium-sized berries, allowing each person 4 berries instead of 3.

cherry-berry cobbler

ESTIMATED PREPARATION TIME: 15 minutes (plus at least 10 minutes cooling time)
COOK TIME: 30 minutes • **SERVINGS:** 9

CONVENIENT INGREDIENTS MAKE this cobbler a snap to put together. You'll be enjoying warm and luscious cobbler in no time! Serve this with Cinnamon Whipped Cream (page 191), if you like.

cooking spray
1 20-ounce can no-sugar-added cherry pie filling (not "light" pie filling)
1 12-ounce package frozen mixed berries, thawed
1 teaspoon vanilla extract
1 tablespoon sugar
1 recipe Low-Carb Cobbler "Biscuit" Topping (page 205)

1. Preheat the oven to 350°F. Spray an 8-inch square baking pan or casserole dish with cooking spray; set aside.
2. In a medium mixing bowl, stir together the pie filling and thawed berries; add the vanilla and sugar and stir well. Spoon mixture into the prepared baking dish. Place cobbler "biscuits" over the top of the fruit mixture, arranging them in three rows of 3 "biscuits" each.
3. Bake for 30 minutes, or until cobbler topping is nicely browned. Remove from the oven and let cool at least 10 minutes before serving.

• APPROXIMATE NUTRITIONAL CONTENT •
Calories: 124, Protein: 8g, Net Carbs: 12g, Fat: 4g, Cholesterol: 8mg, Sodium: 141mg

serving suggestion

Warm cobbler is great with low-carb vanilla ice cream or Homemade Whipped Cream (page 190).

strawberry, cherry, and almond crisp

ESTIMATED PREPARATION TIME: 15 minutes (plus at least 10 minutes cooling time)
COOK TIME: 30 minutes • **SERVINGS:** 9

THE COMBINATION OF both fruits, plus vanilla and almond extracts, makes this crisp especially delicious.

cooking spray
1 20-ounce can no-sugar-added cherry pie filling (not "light" pie filling)
1 12-ounce package frozen strawberries, thawed
½ teaspoon vanilla extract
½ teaspoon almond extract
1 teaspoon sugar
1 recipe Low-Carb Fruit Crisp Topping (page 204)

1. Preheat the oven to 350°F. Spray a 9-inch square baking pan or casserole dish with cooking spray; set aside.
2. In a medium mixing bowl, stir together the pie filling and thawed berries; add the extracts and sugar and stir well.
3. Spoon mixture into the prepared baking dish. Sprinkle topping over the fruit mixture. Bake for 25 to 30 minutes, or until the topping is nicely browned and the fruit is bubbling. Remove from the oven and let cool at least 10 minutes before serving.

• APPROXIMATE NUTRITIONAL CONTENT •
Calories: 139, Protein: 2g, Net Carbs: 13g, Fat: 7g, Cholesterol: 10mg, Sodium: 55mg

layered mandarin cream dessert

ESTIMATED PREPARATION TIME: 20 minutes (plus at least 4 hours chilling time)
COOK TIME: none • **SERVINGS:** 12

A GROWN-UP dessert with wide appeal, this fluffy concoction is a fitting finale for any spring-time meal.

1 cup whipping cream
1/4 cup Grand Marnier liqueur
1/4 cup water
1 3-ounce package split ladyfingers (12 whole ladyfingers)
1 15-ounce can mandarin orange segments, drained, divided
1 2-ounce packet sugar free cheesecake mousse mix (such as Sans Sucre)
3/4 cup low-carb whole milk
1 8-ounce tub mascarpone cheese

1. In a medium mixing bowl, using an electric mixer on medium-high speed, whip the whipping cream until fluffy and makes soft peaks, about 4 minutes; set aside.
2. In a 1-cup measuring cup for liquids, combine the Grand Marnier and the water. Pour mixture into a shallow pan or rimmed plate.
3. Working with 6 ladyfinger halves at a time, lay the ladyfingers in the mixture and flip to soak both sides with the liquid (there should be liquid leftover). Place the ladyfingers into an 8-inch or 9-inch square glass casserole; soak another 6 ladyfinger halves in the liquid remaining in the pan, then place them next to the others in the casserole dish, to make a complete bottom layer. Sprinkle ½ cup of the mandarin segments on top of the ladyfinger layer.
4. In a large mixing bowl, using an electric mixer on medium speed, mix the cheesecake mousse mix with the low-carb milk for 5 minutes, scraping bowl occasionally. Add the mascarpone and mix again to combine well. Add the reserved whipped cream and mix again until mixture is fluffy. Spoon half of the mousse mixture on top of the mandarin segments, and use a rubber spatula to spread the mixture to the edge of the dish. Repeat layers (soaked ladyfingers, mandarin segments, and mousse mixture) once more, keeping out a few mandarin orange segments to garnish the top. Cover the dessert with plastic wrap and refrigerate at least 4 hours before serving.

• APPROXIMATE NUTRITIONAL CONTENT •
Calories: 228, Protein: 4g, Net Carbs: 12g, Fat: 17g, Cholesterol: 59mg, Sodium: 110mg

raspberry-lime fool

ESTIMATED PREPARATION TIME: 10 minutes
COOK TIME: none • **SERVINGS:** 4

A FOOL IS an old-fashioned whipped cream and fruit dessert. I like the updated combination of raspberry and lime, but the more traditional strawberry and lemon is nice, too. You can vary the ingredients any way you like, using any berry you wish, along with a contrasting flavor (frequently citrus).

1 cup whipping cream
2 tablespoons Splenda Granular sweetener
½ teaspoon grated lime peel
1 half-pint container fresh raspberries (about 1 cup)

1. In a medium mixing bowl, using an electric mixer on medium-high speed, whip the cream, Splenda, and lime peel until very stiff.
2. Using a whisk, mix in the raspberries until well blended with the cream. Divide into individual dessert bowls and serve immediately, or cover and chill up to 2 hours.

• **APPROXIMATE NUTRITIONAL CONTENT** •
Calories: 127, Protein: 1g, Net Carbs: 5g, Fat:11g, Cholesterol:41mg, Sodium: 12mg

fresh berry ambrosia

ESTIMATED PREPARATION TIME: 10 minutes
COOK TIME: none • **SERVINGS:** 6

THIS VERSION OF a classic fruit salad tastes remarkably similar to what you may have eaten as a child, but it uses fiber-rich (and lower-carb) fresh berries instead of fruit cocktail, and it's marshmallow-free (but I promise you won't miss them). Use the extra pudding mix to make a single-serve of pudding for yourself by mixing it with about one cup of low-carb milk.

for the cream:

¼ cup water
2 tablespoons Splenda
1½ teaspoons coconut extract
½ cup unsweetened coconut milk
2 tablespoons plus ½ teaspoon sugar-free, fat-free white chocolate pudding mix
⅓ cup low-carb whole milk

1 cup sliced, fresh strawberries
1 half-pint container fresh raspberries (about 1 cup)
1 half-pint container fresh blueberries (about 1 cup)
1 8-ounce can crushed pineapple (juice-packed), well-drained
⅓ cup unsweetened coconut

1. *To make the cream:* In a small mixing bowl, using a whisk, combine the water, Splenda, coconut extract, and coconut milk until blended. Whisk in the pudding mix and milk until mixture is smooth and creamy; set aside.
2. In a medium mixing bowl, gently stir together the fresh fruit, crushed pineapple, and coconut. Using a wooden spoon, stir the cream mixture into the fruit mixture, stirring gently until well combined. Serve immediately or refrigerate until serving time. Stir gently before serving.

• **APPROXIMATE NUTRITIONAL CONTENT** •
Calories: 116, Protein: 2g, Net Carbs: 10.5g, Fat: 6g, Cholesterol: 2mg, Sodium: 125mg

schaum torte

ESTIMATED PREPARATION TIME: 15 minutes (plus at least 1 hour cooling time)
COOK TIME: 45 minutes • **SERVINGS:** 6

MY MOTHER TOLD me that she and her sister used to order Schaum Torte for dessert on those rare occasions when they ate at a restaurant. To me, this old-fashioned treat is a welcome alternative to traditional shortcake. My version includes whipped cream, which is not traditional but makes for a more festive dessert. If you've got locally grown strawberries, all the better (you'll need about one quart).

for the meringue:
4 egg whites, at room temperature
¾ cup plus 1 tablespoon Splenda Granular sweetener
1 teaspoon vanilla extract
⅓ cup Expert Foods' Cake-ability
⅔ cup almond meal/flour (or very finely ground almonds)

2 tablespoons Smucker's sugar-free "light" strawberry preserves
1 16-ounce package fresh strawberries, quartered
1 recipe Homemade Whipped Cream (page 190)

1. *To make the meringue:* Preheat the oven to 250°F. In a large mixing bowl, using an electric mixer on medium-high speed, mix the egg whites until stiff but not dry, about 4 minutes. Add the Splenda, vanilla, and Cake-ability and mix again, on medium speed, until blended and smooth, about 4 more minutes. Using a wooden spoon, stir in the almond meal until incorporated (do not over-stir or egg whites will deflate).

2. Line a cookie sheet with parchment paper. On the parchment, using a pencil, draw two 8-inch-diameter circles. Using the wooden spoon, divide the meringue mixture between the circles, spreading it about 1 inch thick. Bake the meringue for about 45 minutes, or until dry to the touch and crisp. Turn off the oven and let the meringue cool in the oven with the door closed for at least 1 hour before assembling the dessert. (Meringue may be kept at room temperature, uncovered, for several hours or overnight, if desired. If it gets soft or sticky before you assemble the dessert, re-crisp it in a 300°F oven for about 10 minutes).

3. While waiting for the meringue to cool, heat the preserves in a microwavable bowl for about 30 seconds on MEDIUM power, until melted. In a medium bowl, stir together the preserves and strawberries until combined.

4. To assemble the torte: Carefully peel the parchment from the meringue rounds. Place one round on a serving plate. Spoon the whipped cream over the round, spreading it to cover the meringue. Top with the strawberries (it's okay if they spill over the edge of the cream: it will look pretty.) Top with the second meringue round and press down slightly. Serve immediately. (To serve, cut into wedges with a serrated knife and serve with a spatula.)

• APPROXIMATE NUTRITIONAL CONTENT •

Calories: 396, Protein: 10g, Net Carbs: 10g, Fat: 35g, Cholesterol: 109mg, Sodium: 195mg

pavlova

ESTIMATED PREPARATION TIME: 15 minutes (plus at least 1 hour cooling time)
COOK TIME: 1 hour • **SERVINGS:** 6

THIS IS A low-carb variation of a classic meringue-based dessert named for the famous Russian ballerina. Feel free to vary the flavor of whipped cream used, as well as the fruit mixture, to suit your tastes and the season. Be aware that this meringue shell will not stay white during baking; it becomes a light golden color.

for the meringue:

4 egg whites, at room temperature
¾ cup plus 1 tablespoon Splenda Granular sweetener
1 teaspoon vanilla extract
⅓ cup Expert Foods' Cake-ability
⅔ cup almond meal/flour (or very finely chopped almonds)

1 recipe favorite flavor Fruity Whipped Cream (page 194)

2 cups fresh berries

1. *To make the meringue:* Preheat the oven to 250°F. In a large mixing bowl, using an electric mixer on medium-high speed, mix the egg whites until stiff but not dry, about 4 minutes. Add the Splenda, vanilla extract, and Cake-ability and mix again, on medium speed, until blended and smooth, about 4 more minutes. Using a wooden spoon, stir in the almond meal until incorporated (do not over-stir or egg whites will deflate.)

2. Line a cookie sheet with parchment paper. On the parchment, using a pencil, draw an oval 10 inches long and 6 inches wide. Using the wooden spoon, heap the meringue mixture into the oval, spreading it to fill. Build a "nest" with the meringue, making it higher around the edges and level in the center (edges should be at least 2 inches high).

3. Bake the meringue for about 65 minutes, or until dry to the touch and crisp. Turn off the oven and let the meringue cool in the oven with the door closed for at least 1 hour before assembling the dessert. (Meringue may be kept at room temperature, uncovered, for several hours or overnight, if desired. If it gets soft or sticky before you assemble the dessert, re-crisp it in a 300°F oven for about 10 minutes.)

4. *To assemble the pavlova:* Carefully peel the parchment from the meringue "nest." Place the meringue on a serving platter. Spoon about two-thirds of the Fruity Whipped Cream into the depression in the meringue. Top with the berries, allowing some of them to spill over the sides of the meringue. Top with dollops of the remaining Fruity Whipped Cream. Serve immediately, or refrigerate for up to 2 hours before serving. (To serve, cut into wedges with a serrated knife and serve with a spatula.)

• APPROXIMATE NUTRITIONAL CONTENT •
Calories: 258, Protein: 9g, Net Carbs: 9g, Fat: 21g, Cholesterol: 54mg, Sodium: 180mg

spiked citrus raspberries

*W*HEN YOU HAVE top-notch ingredients, a simple preparation is all that's needed.

¼ cup Grand Marnier liqueur
2 tablespoons water
2 teaspoons Splenda Granular sweetener
2 teaspoons grated lemon peel
2 half-pint containers raspberries, washed and drained (about 2 cups)
Fresh mint sprigs for garnish

1. In a 1-cup measuring cup for liquids, stir together the liqueur, water, Splenda, and lemon peel until well combined.
2. Place the berries in a small mixing bowl. Pour liqueur mixture over the berries and gently stir to coat them with the liquid. Divide the berries and liquid among four dessert dishes. Garnish each serving with a sprig of fresh mint.

• **APPROXIMATE NUTRITIONAL CONTENT** •
Calories: 53, Protein: 1g, Net Carbs: 6.5g, Fat: 0g, Cholesterol: 0mg, Sodium: 1mg

strawberries with balsamic vinegar

ESTIMATED PREPARATION TIME: 5 minutes (plus at least 3 hours chilling time)
COOK TIME: none • **SERVINGS:** 4

THIS RECIPE MAY sound a little strange to you, but rest assured, you'll love how the tiny amount of vinegar brings out exceptional sweetness in the berries (and no, it doesn't taste "vinegary"). This is an especially good treatment for berries that aren't at the peak of ripeness, or for store-bought berries, because it heightens their flavor and juiciness.

●

1 16-ounce package strawberries, rinsed, hulled, and quartered
1 tablespoon Splenda Granular sweetener
1 teaspoon good-quality balsamic vinegar
1 teaspoon grated lemon peel
¾ cup Homemade Whipped Cream (page 190)

●

1. In a medium mixing bowl, gently stir all ingredients together (except for the whipped cream). Cover and refrigerate at least 3 hours, to allow berries to develop flavors and juice.
2. To serve, stir berries and divide among individual dessert bowls. Garnish each portion with a dollop of Homemade Whipped Cream.

• APPROXIMATE NUTRITIONAL CONTENT •
Calories: 127, Protein: 1g, Net Carbs: 5g, Fat: 11g, Cholesterol: 41mg, Sodium: 12mg

seasonal specialties

pumpkin pie

ESTIMATED PREPARATION TIME: 15 minutes (plus at least 5 hours cooling/chilling time)
COOK TIME: 40 minutes • **SERVINGS:** 10

THE FLAVOR OF traditional pumpkin pie, but with much less sugar—and it still has a crust! If you want to lower the carbs even more, you can make this pie sans crust using the variation.

½ cup Splenda Granular sweetener
¼ cup Sugar Twin brown sugar substitute
1 teaspoon cinnamon
½ teaspoon ground ginger
¼ teaspoon ground cloves
3 eggs
1 15-ounce can pumpkin (not pumpkin pie mix)
½ cup low-carb whole milk
½ cup whipping cream

1 recipe "Traditional" Pie Crust, partially baked, in a 9-inch pie plate (page 64)
Homemade Whipped Cream, optional garnish (page 190)

1. Preheat oven to 350°F. In a small bowl, stir together the Splenda, Sugar Twin, cinnamon, ginger, and cloves; set aside.

2. In a large mixing bowl, using an electric mixer on medium-low speed, mix the eggs and pumpkin; add the reserved Splenda-spice mixture and mix on medium speed, blending well. Turn the mixer speed down to low and add the milk and whipping cream; blend until smooth.

3. Pour mixture into the partially baked crust, and bake for 40 minutes, or until the pie is set and the center no longer jiggles when the pie is gently shaken. Let the pie cool completely (about 1 hour), then refrigerate for at least 4 hours before serving. Garnish chilled pie with Homemade Whipped Cream before serving, if desired.

• APPROXIMATE NUTRITIONAL CONTENT •
Calories: 187, Protein: 8g, Net Carbs: 9g, Fat: 12g, Cholesterol: 103mg, Sodium: 39mg

INDIVIDUAL CRUSTLESS PUMPKIN "PIES"

Spray six 6-ounce custard cups or ramekins with cooking spray. Place the cups on a baking sheet. Prepare the pumpkin filling mixture as per recipe above. Divide the filling among the custard cups. Bake the cups at 350°F for 25 to 30 minutes, or until set. Let the "pies" cool for 1 hour, then refrigerate at least 2 hours before serving.

• APPROXIMATE NUTRITIONAL CONTENT •
Calories: 145, Protein: 6g, Net Carbs: 4.5g, Fat: 11g, Cholesterol: 137mg, Sodium: 65mg

maple crème brûlée

ESTIMATED PREPARATION TIME: 10 minutes (plus at least 6 hours chilling time)
COOK TIME: 10 minutes • SERVINGS: 6

FOR MANY PEOPLE, including myself crème brûlée was always a restaurant dessert. I thought it must surely be difficult or time-consuming to prepare—it's neither, although it does take a while to chill. This version, full of rich maple flavor, is nice on a fall evening and also makes a good alternate dessert for Thanksgiving.

2 cups light cream
¼ cup Splenda Granular sweetener
2 tablespoons real maple syrup (not sugar-free)
2 teaspoons maple extract
7 egg yolks
12 teaspoons real brown sugar, divided

1. Preheat the oven to 325°F. In a medium saucepan, over medium heat, whisk together the cream and Splenda. Bring mixture to a simmer, whisking constantly. Remove from heat and whisk in the maple syrup and extract; set aside.

2. In a medium mixing bowl, using a whisk, break up the egg yolks slightly (no need to whip them at all). Slowly whisk in the reserved cream mixture until blended. Position a fine sieve over a plastic pitcher; pour the mixture into the pitcher through the sieve to strain it.

3. Place six 4-ounce custard cups or ramekins into a baking pan. Add about 1 inch of hot water to the pan (take care not to get it into the cups). Carefully pour the crème brûlée mixture into the custard cups, dividing it evenly among them.

4. Transfer the pan to the oven and bake for 45 minutes, or until the center of the custards jiggle just slightly when the pan is gently shaken. Remove the custards from the water bath and let them cool on the counter to room temperature. Cover with plastic wrap and refrigerate at least 6 hours (or up to 2 days).

5. When ready to serve, sprinkle 2 teaspoons of brown sugar over each portion, spreading it gently with your fingers to make a thin, even layer. Position the oven rack about 4 inches below the broiler; set oven to medium-broil. Place the custards on a baking sheet and broil about 1 minute, or until the sugar is melted, golden brown, and bubbling. Keep your eye on it; it burns quickly. Remove from

the broiler and let the custards sit at room temperature to allow the sugar to harden to a "crust" before serving.

• APPROXIMATE NUTRITIONAL CONTENT •
Calories: 264, Protein: 5g, Net Carbs: 13g, Fat: 22g, Cholesterol: 302mg, Sodium: 43mg

hazelnut sponge roll with cream filling

ESTIMATED PREPARATION TIME: 15 minutes (plus 2½ hours cooling/chilling time)
COOK TIME: 12 minutes • **SERVINGS:** 10

I'LL ADMIT, IT took me years to work up the nerve to make a cake roll, but once I'd done it, I wondered why I'd waited so long—the results were that good, and that impressive! So, even though this cake takes a little skill and effort, don't be afraid to try it.

for the cake roll:

cooking spray
1 tablespoon all-purpose flour
5 eggs, separated
1 tablespoon Atkins Sugar-Free Hazelnut Syrup
½ teaspoon salt
⅓ cup Splenda Granular sweetener
2 tablespoons brown sugar
¼ cup cornstarch
1 teaspoon baking powder
¾ cup toasted hazelnuts, ground, divided

for the cream filling:

1 8-ounce package cream cheese, softened
3 tablespoons Atkins Sugar-Free Hazelnut Syrup
1½ cups whipping cream
⅓ cup Splenda Granular sweetener

1. Preheat the oven to 375°F. Lightly coat a 10½-by-15½-inch jelly roll pan with cooking spray. Cover the pan with parchment paper or waxed paper (the cooking spray helps the paper stick to the pan and stay in place). Heavily coat the parchment paper with cooking spray, then sprinkle the paper with flour.

2. *To make the cake roll:* In a small bowl, stir together the egg yolks and the hazelnut syrup; set aside. In a medium mixing bowl, using an electric mixer, whip the egg whites on high speed until foamy. Add the salt and beat again until the eggs form soft peaks. Turn the mixer speed down to medium and mix in the Splenda and brown sugar; turn the mixer speed back up to high and continue to beat until mixture is stiff, but not dry.

3. Pour the reserved yolk mixture over the egg white mixture and sprinkle with the cornstarch, baking powder, and ½ cup of the ground nuts. Using a wooden spoon, gently stir until all ingredients are blended (try not to over-stir, which will case the egg whites to deflate). Spread the batter in the prepared pan, smoothing the top with a rubber spatula. Bake cake for 12 minutes, or until lightly browned, and cake springs back when touched lightly in the center.

4. While cake is baking, spread a clean kitchen towel or tea towel on the counter. Sprinkle the towel with the remaining ¼ cup of ground hazelnuts; using clean hands, spread the nuts evenly over the towel. When cake is done baking, remove it from the oven and immediately invert it onto the prepared towel. Carefully peel off the parchment and use a sharp knife to trim any crisp or uneven edges.

5. Gently roll the cake up in the towel, starting from a long edge (the towel will be rolled up inside the cake—that's okay!). Let the cake rest, rolled up in the towel, for 3 minutes, then unroll it and let it rest about 3 minutes more. Roll it up again and let the cake cool completely, about ½ hour. While waiting for the cake to cool, prepare the cream filling.

6. *To prepare the cream filling:* In a medium mixing bowl, using an electric mixer, beat the cream cheese and hazelnut syrup on medium speed until smooth. Add the whipping cream and Splenda, turn the mixer speed to medium-high, and beat until thick and fluffy, about 4 minutes. Refrigerate cream until you're ready to finish the cake.

7. When cake is cool, unroll it and spread with the filling, using a rubber spatula. Leave about ½-inch border clear of filling, all around the edge (this helps keep the filling from leaking out when you roll it back up). Roll the cake up again (this time without the towel inside), and place the roll on a platter. Refrigerate the roll for at least 2 hours, lightly covered with plastic wrap. To serve, use a serrated knife and cut the roll into 10 equal slices.

• **APPROXIMATE NUTRITIONAL CONTENT** •
Calories: 313, Protein: 7g, Net Carbs: 7g, Fat: 29g, Cholesterol: 180mg, Sodium: 269mg

pumpkin cheesecake

ESTIMATED PREPARATION TIME: 15 minutes (plus at least 5 hours cooling/chilling time)
COOK TIME: 55 minutes • **SERVINGS:** 8

THIS DELICIOUS CONCOCTION has all the flavor of traditional pumpkin pie, but in a "company's coming" cheesecake.

for the crust:

cooking spray

5 large graham cracker rectangles, crushed (about ¾ cup crumbs)

2 tablespoons butter, melted

for the cheese filling:

2 8-ounce packages cream cheese, softened

2 eggs

¼ cup whipping cream

⅔ cup canned pumpkin (not pumpkin pie mix)

½ cup Splenda Granular sweetener

1 teaspoon cinnamon

1 teaspoon ground cloves

½ teaspoon ground ginger

1 recipe Cinnamon Whipped Cream (page 191)

1. Preheat the oven to 350°F.
2. *To make the crust:* Spray the bottom and sides of an 8-inch springform pan with cooking spray. In a small bowl, combine the graham cracker crumbs with the melted butter. Pat the mixture into the bottom of the pan, forming an even, but thin crust. Bake crust 5 minutes; remove from oven to cool, but leave oven on. While crust is cooling, prepare cheese filling.
3. *To make the cheese filling:* In a large mixing bowl, using an electric mixer on medium speed, mix together the softened cheese and the eggs, scraping bowl occasionally, until smooth. Add the whipping cream and pumpkin and mix until almost fluffy, about 5 minutes. In a small bowl, combine the Splenda and the spices; add the spice mixture to the cream cheese mixture and mix again to combine thoroughly.

4. Pour filling into cooled crust. Cover the top of the pan with foil, tenting it slightly in the middle so the cake doesn't touch the foil when it rises during baking. Bake 55 minutes. Remove cake from oven and lift off foil. Let cake cool 1 hour, run a knife around the edge to loosen the cake, then refrigerate for at least 4 hours.
5. After cake has chilled, remove the ring from around the pan. Before serving, spread the Cinnamon Whipped Cream over the cheesecake, filling the depression in the middle.

• APPROXIMATE NUTRITIONAL CONTENT •
Calories: 426, Protein: 8g, Net Carbs: 12g, Fat:39g, Cholesterol: 174mg, Sodium: 296mg

cranberry-orange fool

OFFERING A VARIETY of desserts—something to suit everyone—is a great way to end any holiday celebration. This fluffy whipped-cream dessert will please your low-carbing guests, and others will enjoy it as an alternative to the heavier, more traditional selections on your dessert table. This recipe doubles easily; for a crowd, serve it in a decorative glass bowl instead of individual dishes.

1 cup whipping cream
1/4 cup Splenda Granular sweetener
1 1/2 teaspoons grated orange peel
1/4 teaspoon cinnamon
1 cup fresh cranberries, chopped
3 tablespoons freshly squeezed orange juice

1. In a medium mixing bowl, using an electric mixer on medium-high speed, whip the cream, Splenda, orange peel, and cinnamon until very stiff.
2. Using a whisk, mix in the chopped cranberries and orange juice until well blended with the cream. Divide among individual dessert bowls and serve immediately, or cover and chill up to 2 hours.

• APPROXIMATE NUTRITIONAL CONTENT •
Calories: 223, Protein: 1g, Net Carbs: 5g, Fat: 22g, Cholesterol: 82mg, Sodium: 23mg

eggnog bread pudding

A WARM AND homey pudding, this makes an appealing brunch offering, as well as a dessert. Feel free to garnish it with Homemade Whipped Cream (page 190) or Rum Whipped Cream (page 195), if you prefer.

cooking spray
1½ cups dairy eggnog (not "light")
1 cup low-carb whole milk
2 eggs
1 teaspoon vanilla extract
⅓ cup Splenda Granular sweetener
¾ teaspoon nutmeg, divided
6 slices "light" raisin bread, crusts trimmed, cut into 1-inch cubes (slightly staled bread is best)
6 slices low-carb white bread, crusts trimmed, cut into 1-inch cubes (slightly staled bread is best)

1. Spray a 9-inch square casserole dish with cooking spray; set aside. Preheat oven to 325°F. In a medium mixing bowl, combine the eggnog, milk, eggs, vanilla, Splenda, and ½ teaspoon of the nutmeg; whisk until well blended.
2. Add the bread cubes to the mixture and stir until all cubes are coated with the mixture. Let mixture sit for 15 minutes, pressing down on the bread cubes occasionally with a wooden spoon or clean hand, so that all bread is well soaked with the mixture. Stir the mixture once, then pour it into the prepared casserole dish.
3. Bake 55 to 60 minutes, until pudding is nicely browned on top and does not jiggle when the pan is gently shaken. Remove from oven and let cool at least 15 minutes before serving.

• APPROXIMATE NUTRITIONAL CONTENT •
Calories: 195, Protein: 13g, Net Carbs: 14g, Fat: 8g, Cholesterol: 76mg, Sodium: 255mg

peppermint brownie pie

ESTIMATED PREPARATION TIME: 20 minutes (plus at least 3 hours cooling/chilling time)
COOK TIME: 40 minutes • **SERVINGS:** 10

THIS DELICIOUS COMBINATION of brownie, pink peppermint cheesecake, and dark chocolate drizzle makes for a beautiful dessert appropriate for Christmas or Valentine's Day. It looks complicated, but each layer comes together quickly and easily; just allow enough time to assemble it. If you're not a fan of food coloring, feel free to omit it; you'll end up with a sophisticated black-and-white look.

for the brownie layer:

cooking spray
1 8½-ounce package Atkins Fudge Brownie Mix
1 egg
⅓ cup oil
⅓ cup cold water

for the peppermint cheesecake layer:

1 8-ounce package Neufchâtel cheese, softened
¼ cup whipping cream
1 egg
¼ cup Splenda
1 teaspoon peppermint extract
red food coloring

for the chocolate drizzle:

½ ounce sugar-free dark chocolate, chopped
½ teaspoon shortening
½ teaspoon whipping cream

4 sugar-free peppermint hard candies, crushed, for garnish

1. Preheat the oven to 350°F.
2. *To make the brownie layer:* Spray a 9-inch, deep-dish pie plate with cooking spray; set aside. In a medium mixing bowl, using a wooden spoon, combine the brownie mix, egg, oil, and water and stir to combine thoroughly. Spread the batter over

the bottom of the pie plate using a rubber spatula. Bake for 25 to 28 minutes. Remove from oven and let cool completely on a wire rack, about 1 hour. While the brownie layer is cooling, prepare the cheesecake layer.

3. *To make the cheesecake layer:* In a medium mixing bowl, using an electric mixer on medium speed, mix the Neufchâtel cheese, whipping cream, and egg together until blended and smooth, about 2 minutes. Add the Splenda and extract; mix again to combine. Add a few drops of red food coloring to tint the mixture pink and mix again, adding more until it reaches the desired shade of pink.

4. Preheat again to 350°F. Using a rubber spatula, spread the mixture over the brownie layer. Return pie to the oven and bake for 15 minutes, or until set. Remove from the oven and let cool 15 minutes, then chill 1½ hours in the refrigerator.

5. *To make the chocolate drizzle:* In a microwaveable bowl, combine the chopped chocolate, shortening, and whipping cream. Microwave on LOW power for 1 minute, or until chocolate is melted; stir until smooth and combined. Using the spoon, drizzle the mixture over the top of the chilled pie in a decorative fashion. Return pie to the refrigerator for at least ½ hour more before serving.

6. To serve, cut the pie into 8 wedges and place on individual dessert plates using a pie server; sprinkle a bit of the crushed peppermint candy over each piece and serve immediately. (The crushed peppermint candies will "melt" if left on the pie, so it's best to sprinkle them over each piece just before serving, and not over the entire pie.)

• **APPROXIMATE NUTRITIONAL CONTENT** •
Calories: 232, Protein: 5g, Net Carbs: 12g, Fat: 16g, Cholesterol: 69mg, Sodium: 194mg

chocolate-raspberry tartlets

• •

ESTIMATED PREPARATION TIME: 15 minutes (plus at least 1 hour chilling time)
COOK TIME: 3 minutes • **SERVINGS:** 15 (1 tartlet per serving)

• •

THESE BEAUTIFUL TARTLETS get a double dose of raspberry flavor—from the filling and the fresh berry garnish. They are easy to prepare and would make a nice addition to a holiday dessert buffet, hence the small serving size. If you'd rather serve them on their own at a sit-down dinner, allow 3 tartlets per person.

for the filling:

¼ cup whipping cream
1 ounce sugar-free dark chocolate, chopped
8 pieces Russell Stover sugar-free Raspberry Miniatures, chopped
2 teaspoons Smucker's sugar-free, "light" raspberry preserves
½–¾ teaspoon Expert Foods' ThickenThin Not/Starch

1 2.1-ounce package frozen phyllo cups, thawed 10 minutes at room temperature
1 cup Homemade Whipped Cream (page 190) (optional garnish)
15 fresh raspberries (about ½ cup)

1. *To make the filling:* In a small microwavable bowl, heat the cream on LOW power for about 1 minute, until it just comes to a simmer. Stir in the chopped dark chocolate and chopped raspberry chocolates until smooth. Stir in the preserves and thickener until blended and smooth; set aside to thicken.

2. Leave the phyllo cups in their plastic trays. Fill each phyllo cup using a small spoon (do not overfill the cups). Place the tray of filled tartlets in the refrigerator for at least 1 hour, or until serving time.

3. Before serving, garnish each tartlet with a small dollop of Homemade Whipped Cream (if using) and a fresh raspberry. Transfer the tartlets to a serving tray, or to individual dessert plates.

• **APPROXIMATE NUTRITIONAL CONTENT** •
Calories: 69, Protein: 1g, Net Carbs: 3g, Fat: 4g, Cholesterol: 6mg, Sodium: 14mg

eggnog tiramisu

● ●

ESTIMATED PREPARATION TIME: 20 minutes (plus at least 4 hours chilling time)
COOK TIME: none • **SERVINGS:** 12

● ●

THIS IS AN innovative way to feature eggnog on your holiday menu. Although eggnog is not a low-carb beverage, using it as an ingredient in the tiramisu "stretches it out," making it more acceptable for low-carb diets—without sacrificing anything flavor-wise.

●

1 cup eggnog, divided
½ cup low-carb 2% milk
1 1.4-ounce package sugar-free, fat-free white chocolate instant pudding mix
1 8-ounce tub mascarpone cheese, softened
1½ tablespoons dark rum
1 cup Homemade Whipped Cream (page 190)
1 3-ounce package split ladyfingers (12 whole ladyfingers)
¼ teaspoon nutmeg, divided

●

1. In a large mixing bowl, using an electric mixer on medium speed, mix ½ cup of the eggnog with the milk and pudding mix until well combined, scraping sides of bowl with a rubber spatula occasionally. Add the mascarpone and rum and mix until smooth. Whisk the Homemade Whipped Cream into the mixture until blended; set aside.

2. Pour half of the remaining eggnog into a shallow pan or rimmed plate. Working with 6 ladyfinger halves at a time, lay the ladyfingers in the eggnog and flip to soak both sides with the eggnog (there should be liquid left over). Place the ladyfingers into the bottom of an 8-inch or 9-inch square glass casserole; soak another 6 ladyfinger halves in the liquid remaining in the dish, then place them next to the others in the casserole dish, to make a complete bottom layer.

3. Using a rubber spatula, carefully spread half the reserved pudding mixture over the soaked ladyfingers, spreading to the edge of the casserole dish. Sprinkle with ⅛ teaspoon nutmeg. Pour the last of the eggnog into the shallow pan and repeat the layers (soaked ladyfingers, pudding mixture, nutmeg). Cover the tiramisu with plastic wrap and refrigerate for at least 4 hours before serving.

• **APPROXIMATE NUTRITIONAL CONTENT** •
Calories: 219, Protein: 4g, Net Carbs: 11g, Fat: 18g, Cholesterol: 69mg, Sodium: 195mg

gingerbread cheesecake

ESTIMATED PREPARATION TIME: 15 minutes (plus at least 5 hours cooling/chilling time)
COOK TIME: 55 minutes • **SERVINGS:** 10

ƐASIER THAN ROLLING out gingerbread cookies, and lots of great molasses and ginger flavor!

for the crust:
cooking spray
10 gingersnap cookies, crushed fine (about ¾ cup crumbs)
2 tablespoons butter, melted

for the cheese filling:
1 8-ounce package Neufchâtel cheese, softened
1 8-ounce package cream cheese, softened
2 eggs
½ cup whipping cream
2 tablespoons molasses
½ cup Splenda Granular sweetener
1 teaspoon ground ginger
1 teaspoon cinnamon
¼ teaspoon ground cloves
pinch of nutmeg

for the topping:
1 cup Homemade Whipped Cream (page 190)
½ teaspoon vanilla extract
pinch of nutmeg, garnish

1. Preheat the oven to 350°F.
2. *To make the crust:* Spray the bottom and sides of an 8-inch springform pan with cooking spray. In a small bowl, combine the gingersnap crumbs with the melted butter. Pat the mixture into the bottom of the pan, forming an even, but thin crust. Bake crust 5 minutes; remove from oven to cool, but leave oven on. While crust is cooling, prepare cheese filling.

3. *To make the cheese filling:* In a large mixing bowl, using an electric mixer on medium speed, mix together the softened cheeses and the eggs, scraping bowl occasionally, until smooth. Add the whipping cream and molasses, and mix until almost fluffy, about 5 minutes. In a small bowl, combine the Splenda and the spices. Add to the cream cheese mixture and mix to combine thoroughly.

4. Pour filling into cooled crust. Cover the top of the pan with foil, tenting it slightly in the middle so the cake doesn't touch the foil when it rises during baking. Bake 55 minutes. Remove cake from oven and lift off foil. Let cake cool 1 hour, run a knife around edge to loosen cake, and refrigerate for at least 4 hours.

5. After the cake has chilled, remove the ring from around the pan and prepare the topping: In a small mixing bowl, whisk together the Homemade Whipped Cream and vanilla extract until blended. Using a rubber spatula, spread the cream over the cheesecake, filling the depression in the middle. Sprinkle the top with the nutmeg before serving.

• **APPROXIMATE NUTRITIONAL CONTENT** •
Calories: 340, Protein: 6g, Net Carbs: 11g, Fat: 30g, Cholesterol: 140mg, Sodium: 252mg

holiday gelatin wreath

ESTIMATED PREPARATION TIME: 20 minutes (plus at least 6 hours chilling time)
COOK TIME: none • **SERVINGS:** 10

IF YOU'RE HEADING to a holiday potluck or want to round out your open house buffet, this is the perfect dish. With its festive colors, wreath shape, and cheery cherry garnish, it'll perk up any party. As with all molded desserts, the longer you chill it, the better it turns out; feel free to make this a day ahead of time (keep it covered with plastic wrap).

cooking spray

for the green layer:
2 3-ounce packages sugar-free lime gelatin

for the white layer:
1 packet unflavored gelatin
6 ounces (¾ cup) sugar-free lemon-lime soda, divided
¾ cup sour cream
1 cup mini marshmallows

for the red layer:
2 3-ounce packages sugar-free cherry gelatin

¾ cup nondairy whipped topping
5 maraschino cherries, drained, cut in half and blotted dry with paper towel, for garnish

1. Lightly spray a 6-cup, ring-shaped gelatin mold with cooking spray; set aside.
2. *To make the green layer:* In a small bowl, combine 1 cup boiling water with both packages of lime gelatin; stir 1 minute. Add 1 cup cold water and stir another 2 minutes, or until the gelatin is completely dissolved. Pour into the prepared ring mold and refrigerate for 2 hours. When the green gelatin layer is set, prepare the white layer.
3. *To make the white layer:* In a medium bowl, combine the unflavored gelatin with ½ cup of the soda; stir 1 minute. In a microwavable measuring cup for liquids, microwave the remaining ¼ cup soda on HIGH for 1 minute, or until it boils. Stir the boiling soda into the gelatin-soda mixture; stir 2 minutes or until gelatin is

completely dissolved. With a whisk, stir in the sour cream until no lumps remain. Refrigerate in the bowl for 15 to 20 minutes, or until slightly thickened but not set. Stir in the mini-marshmallows and pour mixture over the chilled green layer. Return the gelatin mold to the refrigerator for 2 hours. When the white layer is set, prepare the red layer.

4. *To make the red layer:* In a small bowl, combine 1 cup boiling water with both packages of cherry gelatin; stir 1 minute. Add 1 cup cold water and stir another 2 minutes, or until the gelatin is completely dissolved. Refrigerate the bowl for 15 to 20 minutes to chill it, then pour the cherry gelatin over the white layer of the gelatin mold and refrigerate at least 2 hours before serving.

5. To unmold the gelatin, run a paring knife around the edge of the gelatin to loosen the top. Dip the pan into a large bowlful (or sinkful) of warm water until the water comes halfway up the sides of the mold; hold 20 seconds. (Be careful not to get any water onto the gelatin.) Remove mold from water and place a serving platter over the top of the mold, then invert the gelatin onto the plate. Shake gently to loosen it from the mold. If it doesn't come out easily, repeat the dipping Process for another 10 seconds and try again.

6. Garnish the top of the gelatin wreath with 10 piped rosettes (or small dollops) of whipped topping, spaced evenly around the wreath. Top each rosette with a maraschino cherry half. Cut wreath into 10 slices and serve.

• APPROXIMATE NUTRITIONAL CONTENT •
Calories: 91, Protein: 4g, Net Carbs: 8g, Fat: 5g, Cholesterol: 8mg, Sodium: 103mg

easy easter mosaic gelatin

ESTIMATED PREPARATION TIME: 10 minutes (plus at least 5 hours chilling time)
COOK TIME: none • **SERVINGS:** 6

FEATURING EASTER COLORS and a light lemon flavor, this gelatin mold will complement any holiday dinner.

cooking spray
2 3-ounce packages sugar-free lemon gelatin
¾ cup sour cream
¼ cup nondairy whipped topping
1½ cups multicolored, fruit-flavored miniature marshmallows

1. Lightly spray a 4-cup gelatin mold with cooking spray; set aside. In a medium mixing bowl, combine 1½ cups boiling water with both packages of lemon gelatin; stir 1 minute. Add ¾ cup cold water and stir another 2 minutes, or until the gelatin is completely dissolved. Refrigerate in the mixing bowl for 2 hours, or until gelatin becomes thick but not set. (Test by putting 1 miniature marshmallow into the bowl and stirring it in. If the marshmallow doesn't float, the gelatin is ready.)

2. Stir in the miniature marshmallows, then spoon the mixture into the prepared gelatin mold. Refrigerate at least 3 more hours, or until gelatin is completely set and firm.

3. To unmold the gelatin, dip the pan into a large bowlful of warm water until the water comes halfway up the sides of the mold; hold 20 seconds. (Be careful not to get any water onto the gelatin.) Remove mold from water and place a serving platter over the top of the mold, then invert the gelatin onto the plate. Shake gently to loosen the gelatin from the mold. If it doesn't come out easily, repeat the dipping process for another 10 seconds and try again. Cut gelatin into six portions and serve.

• **APPROXIMATE NUTRITIONAL CONTENT** •
Calories: 121, Protein: 3g, Net Carbs: 12g, Fat: 7g, Cholesterol: 13mg, Sodium: 100mg

tangy citrus-coconut tart

ESTIMATED PREPARATION TIME: 10 minutes (plus at least 3 hours chilling time)
COOK TIME: 10 minutes, plus 8 minutes for crust • **SERVINGS:** 10

*W*ITH JUST ENOUGH sweetness to balance the tangy lemon and lime flavors, this tart makes a cool and refreshing finish to a springtime meal. If you'd rather use low-carb thickener (such as ThickenThin Not/Starch), be aware that the filling will turn creamy, which isn't as pretty as a clear filling such as this; it takes about 3 tablespoons to thicken the filling.

for the citrus filling:

$2/3$ cup fresh lemon juice
$1/4$ cup fresh lime juice
1 cup water
1 cup Splenda Granular sweetener
$1/4$ cup cornstarch
$1/4$ teaspoon salt
4 egg yolks, slightly beaten
1 tablespoon butter

2 tablespoons unsweetened coconut, toasted

1 recipe Coconut-Shortbread Cookie Crust (page 66), baked in a 7-by-11-inch rectangular tart pan with a removable bottom (or a 9-inch pan with removable bottom), and cooled

1. In a small, heavy saucepan, over medium heat, whisk together the juices, water, Splenda, cornstarch, and salt until all ingredients are dissolved together. Continue to whisk constantly until mixture thickens and becomes clear, about 7 minutes. Turn off the heat and quickly whisk in the egg yolks until well combined. Turn the heat back on to medium and cook another 2 minutes until mixture thickens even more.

2. Remove pan from heat and whisk in the butter until melted and mixture is smooth. Let filling cool 5 minutes before pouring it into the crust. Smooth and spread the citrus filling to the edges with a rubber spatula.

3. Sprinkle the tart with the toasted coconut to garnish. Refrigerate tart at least 3 hours, then remove pan edge before serving.

• APPROXIMATE NUTRITIONAL CONTENT •
Calories: 175, Protein: 2g, Net Carbs: 10g, Fat: 14g, Cholesterol: 104mg, Sodium: 171mg

red, white, and blue berry tart

ESTIMATED PREPARATION TIME: 25 minutes (plus at least 2 hours chilling time)
COOK TIME: none • **SERVINGS:** 10

THIS BEAUTIFUL TART, decorated with summer berries, features a citrus-spiked cream cheese filling and a crunchy gingersnap crust. It's a favorite make-ahead dessert for Fourth of July barbeques. Feel free to use just one type of berry, or to use blackberries and sliced strawberries, as the topping.

for the crust:

cooking spray
10 gingersnaps, crushed (about ¾ cup crumbs)
½ cup almond meal/flour (or very finely chopped almonds)
2 large graham cracker rectangles, crushed (about ¼ cup crumbs)
4 tablespoons butter, melted

for citrus cream filling:

1 8-ounce package cream cheese, softened
½ cup whipping cream
3 tablespoons Splenda Granular sweetener
2 tablespoons Smucker's sugar-free "light" orange marmalade
1 tablespoon grated lemon peel
1 teaspoon fresh lemon juice
1 teaspoon fresh lime juice

for berry topping:

1 half-pint container fresh raspberries, washed and air-dried on paper towels (about 1 cup)
1 half-pint container resh blueberries, washed and air-dried on paper towels (about 1 cup)

1. Preheat the oven to 350°F.
2. *To make the crust:*. Spray a 9-inch tart pan with a removable bottom with cooking spray; set aside. In a small bowl, combine all crust ingredients. Pat crust mixture into bottom and up the sides of the pan. Bake the crust for 8 minutes, until nicely browned, then let cool completely, about 30 minutes. While crust is cooling, prepare the citrus cream filling.

3. *To make the citrus cream filling:* In a medium mixing bowl, using an electric mixer on medium speed, mix together the cream cheese and whipping cream until blended and smooth, scraping bowl occasionally. Add the remaining filling ingredients and mix until combined, about 2 minutes. Using a rubber spatula, carefully spread the filling onto the cooled crust, smoothing the top. Refrigerate tart for at least 2 hours before serving.

4. Just before serving, remove the tart pan edge and arrange the air-dried berries on top of the filling in a decorative pattern.

• **APPROXIMATE NUTRITIONAL CONTENT** •

Calories: 253, Protein: 4g, Net Carbs: 13g, Fat: 21g, Cholesterol: 54mg, Sodium: 181mg

no-bake orange cheesecake

● ●

ESTIMATED PREPARATION TIME: 15 minutes (plus at least 6 hours chilling time)
COOK TIME: none • **SERVINGS:** 10

● ●

*W*HEN YOU WANT a nice summer cheesecake but don't want to heat up your kitchen, try this recipe. Everyone who tried it thought it tasted "just like a Creamsicle." Plus, it's easy to prepare and uses just a few ingredients. Prefer a different flavor? Use lemon gelatin and lemon extract, cherry gelatin and cherry extract, or lime gelatin and one teaspoon grated lime peel instead of the extract.

●

for the crust:
cooking spray
1 recipe Nutty Graham Crust (page 61)

for the cheese filling:
2 8-ounce packages cream cheese, softened
1 tablespoon lemon juice
1 cup whipping cream
¼ cup Splenda Granular sweetener
1 0.3-ounce package sugar-free orange gelatin
1½ teaspoons orange extract

●

1. *To make the crust:* Spray the bottom and sides of a 9-inch springform pan with cooking spray. Press the Nutty Graham Crust mixture onto the bottom of the pan. Set crust aside while preparing filling.

2. *To make the cheese filling:* In a large mixing bowl, using an electric mixer on medium speed, blend together the softened cheese and the lemon juice, scraping bowl occasionally, until smooth. Add the whipping cream and mix on medium speed until very thick, about 2 minutes. Add the Splenda, gelatin, and orange extract, and mix on high speed until filling nearly doubles in volume and becomes stiff.

3. Transfer filling to the crust, using a rubber spatula to smooth the top. Cover lightly with plastic wrap (don't let the wrap touch the filling surface), and refrigerate at least 6 hours or overnight. After chilling, run a sharp knife around the inside edge of the pan to loosen cake, then remove the ring from around the pan.

• **APPROXIMATE NUTRITIONAL CONTENT** •
Calories: 379, Protein: 11g, Net Carbs: 3g, Fat: 37g, Cholesterol: 99mg, Sodium: 165mg

creamy banana-coconut squares

ESTIMATED PREPARATION TIME: 15 minutes (plus at least 2 hours chilling time)
COOK TIME: none • **SERVINGS:** 12

AN EASY DESSERT that combines two popular tropical flavors—perfect after a Caribbean-style barbeque dinner.

1 cup whipping cream
½ cup unsweetened coconut milk
¼ cup Splenda Granular sweetener
1 1.4-ounce package sugar-free, fat-free banana cream instant pudding mix
1¾ cups low-carb whole milk
1 3-ounce package split ladyfingers (12 whole ladyfingers)
1 tablespoon banana extract
⅓ cup water
2 tablespoons unsweetened coconut, toasted

1. In a medium mixing bowl, using an electric mixer on medium-high speed, whip the whipping cream until it forms soft peaks. Add the coconut milk and Splenda and whip again to blend; set aside.

2. In a small mixing bowl, whisk together the pudding mix and milk until blended. Transfer the pudding mixture to the bowl with the whipped cream and whip both mixtures together using the electric mixer on medium-high speed, until light and fluffy, about 2 minutes.

3. In a 1-cup measuring cup for liquids, stir together the banana extract and water; pour half the mixture into a shallow pan or rimmed plate. Working with 6 ladyfinger halves at a time, lay the ladyfingers in the mixture, and flip to soak both sides with the liquid (there should be liquid left over). Place the ladyfingers into an 8-inch or 9-inch square casserole; soak another 6 ladyfinger halves in the liquid remaining in the pan, then place them next to the others in the casserole dish, to make a complete bottom layer.

4. Using a rubber spatula, carefully spread half the pudding mixture over the soaked ladyfingers, spreading to the edge of the casserole dish. Pour the remaining banana extract liquid into the shallow pan and repeat the layers, ending with pudding mixture on top. Sprinkle with the toasted coconut and refrigerate at least 2 hours. To serve, cut into 12 even squares and lift out servings with a small spatula.

• **APPROXIMATE NUTRITIONAL CONTENT** •
Calories: 141, Protein: 3g, Net Carbs: 7.5g, Fat: 11g, Cholesterol: 45mg, Sodium: 197mg

summer berry trifle

Prep time: 15 minutes (plus at least 6 hours chilling time)
COOK TIME: none • **SERVINGS:** 12

SUMMER CELEBRATIONS DESERVE stunning desserts, and this one is quick, utilizes wonderful summer berries, can be made a day ahead, and requires absolutely no baking! The red, white, and blue color scheme makes it a natural for Memorial Day or Fourth of July cookouts, but if you'd rather use just one type of berry, that's fine, too (you'll need about 4½ cups of berries total).

for the sauce:

1 cup Smucker's sugar-free, "light" strawberry preserves
1 tablespoon lemon juice
1 tablespoon water

for the cream filling:

1 cup whipping cream
1 teaspoon vanilla extract
1 8-ounce package Neufchâtel cheese, softened
½ cup Splenda Granular sweetener

for the fruit mixture:

1 16-ounce container strawberries, hulled and diced
1½ half-pint containers blueberries (about 1½ cups)

1 14-ounce low-carb pound cake, cut into 1-inch cubes (such as Entenmann's)

1. *Prepare the sauce:* In a small microwavable bowl, stir together sauce ingredients until blended. Microwave sauce 2 minutes on MEDIUM power, or until melted, then stir to blend; set aside.
2. *Prepare the cream filling:* In a medium mixing bowl, using an electric mixer on medium-high speed, whip the cream and vanilla extract until stiff peaks form. In another bowl, using an electric mixer on medium speed, mix the Neufchâtel cheese and Splenda until smooth, about 2 minutes. With a wooden spoon, gently stir the whipped-cream mixture into the cheese mixture until combined; set aside.

3. *Prepare the fruit:* In a large bowl, with a wooden spoon, gently mix the berries together and set aside.

4. *To assemble the trifle:* Place one-third of the pound cake in the bottom of an 8-inch round trifle dish or large glass bowl. Top with one-third of the sauce, then one-third of the cream filling, and one-third of the fruit mixture. Repeat layers twice more, ending with fruit on the top. Cover with plastic wrap and chill at least 6 hours, or even overnight.

• APPROXIMATE NUTRITIONAL CONTENT •
Calories: 263, Protein: 5g, Net Carbs: 17g, Fat: 18g, Cholesterol: 85mg, Sodium: 84mg

the
extras

homemade whipped cream

EVEN WITHOUT REAL sugar, nothing compares to real whipped cream. Many recipes in this book rely on this dessert staple as an ingredient or garnish.

1 cup (½ pint) whipping cream
2 tablespoons Splenda Granular sweetener

1. In a medium mixing bowl, using an electric mixer on medium-high speed, whip the cream until it forms soft peaks.
2. Add the Splenda and whip again until the cream becomes light and fluffy. Use immediately or refrigerate until needed.

• **APPROXIMATE NUTRITIONAL CONTENT** •
Calories: 103, Protein: 1g, Net Carbs: 1g, Fat: 11g, Cholesterol: 41mg, Sodium: 11mg

cinnamon whipped cream

ESTIMATED PREPARATION TIME: 5 minutes
COOK TIME: none • **SERVINGS:** 2 cups (8 ¼ cup servings)

THIS TASTY GARNISH is great with fruit; try a dollop on top of fresh strawberries or blueberries, or with Cherry-Berry Cobbler (page 199).

1 cup (½ pint) whipping cream
2 tablespoons Splenda Granular sweetener
1 teaspoon ground cinnamon

1. In a medium mixing bowl, using an electric mixer on medium-high speed, whip the cream until it forms soft peaks.
2. Add the Splenda and cinnamon; whip again until the cream becomes light and fluffy. Use immediately or refrigerate until needed.

• APPROXIMATE NUTRITIONAL CONTENT •
Calories: 103, Protein: 1g, Net Carbs: 1g, Fat: 11g, Cholesterol: 41mg, Sodium: 11mg

maple whipped cream

THE MAPLE SYRUP in this imparts a subtle flavor that's nice for fall or holiday desserts, such as Pumpkin Pie (page 162). If you don't have any syrup handy, use ¼–½ teaspoon maple extract instead, and increase the Splenda to 2 tablespoons.

1 cup (½ pint) whipping cream
1 tablespoon Splenda Granular sweetener
2 tablespoons sugar-free maple syrup

1. In a medium mixing bowl, using an electric mixer on medium-high speed, whip the cream until it forms soft peaks.
2. Add the Splenda and syrup, and whip again until the cream becomes light and fluffy. Use immediately or refrigerate until needed.

• **APPROXIMATE NUTRITIONAL CONTENT** •
Calories: 103, Protein: 1g, Net Carbs: 1g, Fat: 11g, Cholesterol: 41mg, Sodium: 19mg

chocolate whipped cream

ESTIMATED PREPARATION TIME: 5 minutes
COOK TIME: none • **SERVINGS:** 2 cups (8 1/4-cup servings)

THIS IS PERFECT for topping a low-carb sundae, or for garnishing ripe strawberries.

1 cup (1/2 pint) whipping cream
2 tablespoons Splenda Granular sweetener
1 tablespoon unsweetened cocoa powder

1. In a medium mixing bowl, using an electric mixer on medium-high speed, whip the cream until it forms soft peaks.
2. Add the Splenda and cocoa, and whip again until the cream becomes light and fluffy. Use immediately or refrigerate until needed.

• APPROXIMATE NUTRITIONAL CONTENT •
Calories: 104, Protein: 1g, Net Carbs: 1g, Fat: 11g, Cholesterol: 41mg, Sodium: 11mg

fruity whipped cream

ESTIMATED PREPARATION TIME: 5 minutes
COOK TIME: none • **SERVINGS:** 2 cups (8 ¼-cup servings)

A STYLISH ALTERNATIVE to plain whipped cream, this versatile cream can dress up any fruit dessert with extra color and flavor. For an easy parfait, layer Fruity Whipped Cream with your favorite berries in a sundae glass—delicious, easy, and beautiful!

1 cup (½ pint) whipping cream
1 tablespoon Splenda Granular sweetener
3 tablespoons Smucker's sugar-free, "light" preserves (choose a flavor that will accent the dessert you're serving)

1. In a medium mixing bowl, using an electric mixer on medium-high speed, whip the cream until it forms soft peaks.
2. Add the Splenda and preserves, and whip again until the cream becomes light and fluffy. Use immediately or refrigerate until needed.

• APPROXIMATE NUTRITIONAL CONTENT •
Calories: 106, Protein: 1g, Net Carbs: 3g, Fat: 11g, Cholesterol: 41mg, Sodium: 11mg

rum whipped cream

ESTIMATED PREPARATION TIME: 5 minutes
COOK TIME: none • **SERVINGS:** 1 cup (8 2-tablespoon servings)

A GROWN-UP garnish for sure, it's especially tasty on top of Rum-Raisin Bread Pudding (page 120).

●

½ cup whipping cream
1 tablespoon Splenda Granular sweetener
2 teaspoons rum
⅛ teaspoon vanilla extract

●

1. In a medium mixing bowl, using an electric mixer on medium-high speed, whip the cream until it forms soft peaks.
2. Add the Splenda, rum, and vanilla extract, and whip again until the cream becomes light and fluffy. Use immediately or refrigerate until needed.

• APPROXIMATE NUTRITIONAL CONTENT •
Calories: 54, Protein: 0g, Net Carbs: 0g, Fat: 6g, Cholesterol: 20mg, Sodium: 6mg

cream cheese frosting

AN EASY, TASTY frosting that you can use on bar cookies or a single-layer cake.

4 ounces cream cheese, softened
2 tablespoons butter, softened
2 tablespoons Splenda Granular sweetener
1 tablespoon powdered sugar
2 tablespoons whipping cream
1/4 teaspoon vanilla extract

1. In a medium mixing bowl, using an electric mixer on medium speed, mix the cream cheese with the butter, scraping the bowl occasionally, until well blended.
2. Add the remaining ingredients and mix until smooth and creamy. Use immediately or refrigerate until needed.

• **APPROXIMATE NUTRITIONAL CONTENT** •
Calories: 82, Protein: 1g, Net Carbs: 1g, Fat: 8g, Cholesterol: 25mg, Sodium: 65mg

low-carb hot fudge

ESTIMATED PREPARATION TIME: 4 minutes
COOK TIME: 2 minutes • **SERVINGS:** 1/2 cup (4 2-tablespoon servings)

THICK, RICH, WARM fudge can take a dessert from "ho hum" to "oh, yum" in a flash! From cheesecake to ice cream, this fudge will dress up your desserts without adding a single gram of Net Carbss! Refrigerate any leftovers; it can easily be rewarmed in the microwave.

1/4 cup whipping cream
1 tablespoon Splenda Granular sweetener
1 tablespoon water
1/4 teaspoon vanilla extract
1/8 teaspoon instant coffee granules
pinch of salt
3 ounces sugar-free dark chocolate, chopped
1 1/2 ounces sugar-free milk chocolate, chopped

1. In a small microwavable bowl, stir together the whipping cream, Splenda, water, vanilla extract, coffee granules, and salt. Microwave on MEDIUM power for 2 minutes, until mixture comes to a simmer.
2. Remove from the microwave and stir in the chopped chocolate until fudge becomes thick and glossy. Serve immediately.

• **APPROXIMATE NUTRITIONAL CONTENT** •
Calories: 189, Protein: 3g, Net Carbs: 0g, Fat: 16g, Cholesterol: 20mg, Sodium: 120mg

variation

LOW-CARB CHOCOLATE SAUCE

For a thinner sauce, as opposed to a thick fudge, simply increase the whipping cream to 1/2 cup. The yield on this recipe is 1 cup (8 2-tablespoon servings)

• **APPROXIMATE NUTRITIONAL CONTENT** •
Calories: 120, Protein: 1g, Net Carbs: 0g, Fat: 11g, Cholesterol: 20mg, Sodium: 63mg

chocolate glaze

ESTIMATED PREPARATION TIME: 4 minutes
COOK TIME: 2 minutes • **SERVINGS:** ⅓ cup (3 2-tablespoon servings)

I'VE USED THIS glaze throughout the book as a topping, in which case the entire recipe amount is used, such as for Boston Cream Pie (page 20) and Coconut "Joy" Cheesecake (page 32). It may also be used to drizzle over fruit. Refrigerate any leftover glaze; it can easily be softened or rewarmed in the microwave.

2 tablespoons whipping cream
1 tablespoon water
1 teaspoon Splenda Granular sweetener
3 ounces sugar-free chocolate (any combination of milk, dark, or bittersweet), chopped

1. In a small microwavable bowl, stir together the whipping cream, water, and Splenda. Microwave on MEDIUM power for 1½ to 2 minutes, until mixture comes to a simmer.
2. Remove from the microwave and stir in the chopped chocolate until glaze becomes thickened and glossy.

• **APPROXIMATE NUTRITIONAL CONTENT** •
Calories: 153, Protein: 2g, Net Carbs: 0g, Fat: 13g, Cholesterol: 14mg, Sodium: 5mg

---

variations

DARK CHOCOLATE GLAZE: Use only sugar-free dark chocolate in the recipe.
MILK CHOCOLATE GLAZE: Use only sugar-free milk chocolate in the recipe.

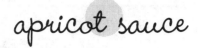

apricot sauce

THIS BEAUTIFUL AND flavorful sauce is wonderful over fresh berries, low-carb ice cream, or over low-carb French toast or pancakes. Using a low-carb thickener would work (and decrease the carbs a little), but it also changes the look of the sauce, making it opaque instead of clear. I like it this way, but you choose what's best for your needs.

1 5.5-ounce can apricot nectar
¼ cup cold water
3 tablespoons Splenda Granular sweetener
1 teaspoon sugar
1 tablespoon cornstarch
½ teaspoon lemon juice

1. In a medium saucepan, over medium-high heat, whisk all ingredients together, except for lemon juice. Bring mixture to a boil, whisking frequently, then cook another 2 minutes, or until the sauce thickens and becomes clear.
2. Remove from heat and stir in ½ teaspoon lemon juice. Let sauce cool to room temperature before serving.

• **APPROXIMATE NUTRITIONAL CONTENT** •
Calories: 17, Protein: 0g, Net Carbs: 4g, Fat: 0g, Cholesterol: 0mg, Sodium: 1mg

easiest fruit sauce

ESTIMATED PREPARATION TIME: 1 minute (plus at least 10 minutes of cooling time)
Cook Time: 4 minutes • **SERVINGS:** 1/2 cup (8 1-tablespoon servings)

PERFECT FOR TOPPING a cheesecake or ice-cream sundae, you'll rely on this recipe frequently to help dress up your desserts. Consider adding some of the suggested spices below, too.

•

1/2 cup sugar-free "light" preserves (such as Smucker's)
1 tablespoon water

•

1. In a small saucepan, over medium heat, whisk the preserves and water together. Add suggested spices or extracts, if desired (see below), and continue to whisk and cook until mixture just comes to a simmer, about 4 minutes.
2. Turn off the heat and let sauce cool 10 minutes before serving it, or using it to top a cheesecake. (This recipe makes enough to top an entire 8-inch cheesecake.)

• **APPROXIMATE NUTRITIONAL CONTENT** •
Calories: 5, Protein: 0g, Net Carbs: 2.5g, Fat: 0g, Cholesterol: 0mg, Sodium: 0mg

suggested sauce combinations

Feel free to use some of these tasty flavor combinations, or create your own!

APRICOT TOPPING: Use apricot preserves and add 1/4 teaspoon almond extract or pinch of nutmeg in Step 1.

BLACKBERRY TOPPING: Use blackberry preserves and add a pinch of cinnamon in Step 1.

CONCORD GRAPE TOPPING: Use concord grape preserves and add 1/4 teaspoon lemon juice in Step 1.

ORANGE MARMALADE TOPPING: Use orange marmalade and add a pinch of cinnamon in Step 1.

RED RASPBERRY TOPPING: Use raspberry preserves and add 1/4 teaspoon vanilla extract in Step 1.

STRAWBERRY TOPPING: Use strawberry preserves and add 1/4 teaspoon lemon juice in Step 1.

raspberry coulis

ESTIMATED PREPARATION TIME: 4 minutes
COOK TIME: none • **SERVINGS:** 2 cups (16 2-tablespoon servings)

RASPBERRY COULIS IS just a fancy name for seedless raspberry sauce. You could use fresh raspberries if you like, but the frozen ones work just as well (and that way you can save the pricey fresh berries for when it really matters). Serve the coulis in a "pool" under Almond Roulade with Raspberry Cream Filling (page 28) or Flourless Chocolate Cake (page 26), or drizzle it over a slice of cheesecake.

2 10-ounce bags frozen, unsweetened raspberries, thawed
¼ cup water
¼ cup fresh lemon juice
2 tablespoons Splenda Granular sweetener
1 tablespoon sugar

1. Add all ingredients to a blender and process about 1 minute, until pureed.
2. Strain mixture though a sieve, over a medium mixing bowl, to remove the seeds and pulp. Press the mixture with the back of a wooden spoon to help force it through the sieve, scooping out the seeds every so often. You should end up with 2 cups of sauce.

• **APPROXIMATE NUTRITIONAL CONTENT** •
Calories: 21, Protein: 0g, Net Carbs: 4g, Fat: 0g, Cholesterol: 0mg, Sodium: 0mg

low-carb crème anglaise

ESTIMATED PREPARATION TIME: 1 minute
COOK TIME: 12 minutes • **SERVINGS:** 1½ cups (12 2-tablespoon servings)

THIS IS A low-carb take on the famous French dessert sauce. It may be unsophisticated to admit, but to me crème anglaise has always tasted like melted vanilla ice cream—delicious! It may be served warm or cold, over fruit or cake. I like it at room temperature over perfectly ripe berries, or "pooled" under Hazelnut Sponge Roll with Cream Filling (page 166).

4 egg yolks
3 tablespoons Splenda Granular sweetener
dash of salt
1½ cups low-carb whole milk
½ teaspoon vanilla extract

1. In a small mixing bowl, whisk the egg yolks until light yellow in color, about 4 minutes. Whisk in Splenda and salt, then add the milk and whisk to blend.
2. Pour about 1½ inches of water in the bottom part of a double boiler (or use two saucepans that fit together but don't touch; put the water in the bottom saucepan). Turn the heat on to medium-high; bring water to a simmer, then lower heat to medium or medium-low, until water is gently simmering (not boiling).
3. Transfer mixture to the top part of the double boiler (or the top saucepan) and cook, stirring constantly with a wooden spoon, for about 10 to 12 minutes, or until sauce has thickened and coats the back of the spoon without dripping off. (Do *not* let the sauce boil; you may have to lower the heat to prevent the sauce from boiling.)
4. Remove from the heat and stir in the vanilla extract. Serve warm, or refrigerate for later use.

• **APPROXIMATE NUTRITIONAL CONTENT** •
Calories: 36, Protein: 2g, Net Carbs: 0g, Fat: 3g, Cholesterol: 75mg, Sodium: 55mg

sweetened crème fraîche

ESTIMATED PREPARATION TIME: 1 minute (plus 24 hours "resting"/chilling time)
COOK TIME: none • **SERVINGS:** about 1 cup (8 2-tablespoon servings)

CRÈME FRAÎCHE IS one of those restaurant-fancy sauces that most people don't make at home because they don't realize how easy it is! Typical crème fraîche is not sweet and is used in a variety of dishes, but this version is sweetened slightly, to make it more "dessert-friendly." Try a dollop over fresh berries.

1 cup whipping cream
2 tablespoons buttermilk
2 tablespoons Sugar Twin brown sugar substitute

1. In a small mixing bowl, whisk together the whipping cream and buttermilk. Cover loosely with plastic wrap and let stand at room temperature for 8 hours.
2. Transfer mixture to the refrigerator to chill and thicken for another 16 hours.
3. Stir in Sugar Twin and serve, or refrigerate until serving time.

• **APPROXIMATE NUTRITIONAL CONTENT** •
Calories: 105, Protein: 1g, Net Carbs: 1g, Fat: 11g, Cholesterol: 41mg, Sodium: 17mg

low-carb fruit crisp topping

ESTIMATED PREPARATION TIME: 5 minutes

COOK TIME: 30 minutes (when baked on fruit crisp) • **SERVINGS:** 9 (enough for an 8-inch or 9-inch square crisp)

THIS EASY TOPPING utilizes packaged low-carb granola, which gives it lots of texture and a little sweetness. Feel free to use your favorite kind of nut in the recipe; I used almond meal, but you could grind up or finely chop hazelnuts, walnuts, or pecans, all of which are appropriate for a fruit crisp.

½ cup low-carb granola (such as MiniCarb)
¼ cup almond meal/flour (or very finely chopped almonds)
2 tablespoons whole wheat flour
3 tablespoons Sugar Twin brown sugar substitute
1 tablespoon sugar
1½ teaspoons cinnamon
3 tablespoons cold butter, diced

1. In a small mixing bowl, using a fork, stir together all the ingredients, except for the butter. Using clean hands, work in the butter until mixture resembles large crumbs.
2. Sprinkle topping mixture over the prepared fruit crisp and bake as directed.

• APPROXIMATE NUTRITIONAL CONTENT •
Calories: 97, Protein: 2g, Net Carbs: 3.5g, Fat: 7g, Cholesterol: 10mg, Sodium: 44mg

low-carb cobbler "biscuit" topping

ESTIMATED PREPARATION TIME: 5 minutes
COOK TIME: about 30 minutes (when baked on fruit cobbler) • **SERVINGS:** 9 "biscuits"
(enough for an 8-inch or 9-inch square cobbler)

THESE TENDER "BISCUITS" are a great topping for any fruit cobbler. For a quick and easy garnish, sprinkle each "biscuit" with a tiny pinch of cinnamon or nutmeg before baking the cobbler. You may also use these "biscuits" as a low-carb shortcake; top with fruit and Homemade Whipped Cream (page 190).

1 cup Atkins Bake Mix
2 tablespoons Splenda Granular sweetener
½ teaspoon cinnamon
2 tablespoons butter, melted
¼ cup low-carb whole milk
3–4 tablespoons hot water

1. In a small mixing bowl, using a fork, stir together the Bake Mix, Splenda, and cinnamon until mixed. Add the butter and milk, and stir again until mixture forms crumbs. Add hot water, a tablespoon at a time, until mixture forms a ball (depending on humidity, not all the water may be used).
2. Shape dough into 9 small disks or "biscuits," about ½ inch thick. Place the biscuits on top of the prepared fruit cobbler mixture and bake as directed in cobbler recipe.

• APPROXIMATE NUTRITIONAL CONTENT •
Calories: 75, Protein: 8g, Net Carbs: 1.5g, Fat: 4g, Cholesterol: 8mg, Sodium: 130mg

acknowledgments

WRITING THIS BOOK has been one of the biggest pleasures of my professional life. While some might credit that solely to the excitement and satisfaction one derives from the creative process itself, I know that without the assistance of the following people, this experience would not have been nearly as wonderful. Thanks to:

- My agent, Lisa Ekus, who championed this idea from the get-go; thanks for your continued assistance and friendship.
- My editor, Sue McCloskey, who believed in this project and me, and who always makes it easy and pleasurable to be a Marlowe author.
- Kim Mayone, my foodie friend and coauthor on previous low-carb books; your helpful (and tactful) comments and suggestions are always on target and always appreciated.
- My neighbors and friends, who tasted, tested, and reviewed recipes; thanks for your help.
- My siblings and parents; no one could ask for better cheerleaders—I love you all.
- My children, Jack and Amelia Scofield, who willingly taste-tested nearly every dessert!
- My husband, Daniel Scofield, who served as a sounding board, taste-tester, and all-around helper. Without you, I wouldn't have the courage, stamina, or time to write; thanks, as always, for your loving support.

—Kitty Broihier

index